Understanding & Response

ROY DYCHE

HEINEMANN
EDUCATIONAL

Heinemann Educational,
a division of Heinemann Educational Books Ltd,
Halley Court, Jordan Hill, Oxford OX2 8EJ

OXFORD LONDON EDINBURGH
MELBOURNE SYDNEY AUCKLAND
IBADAN NAIROBI GABORONE HARARE
KINGSTON PORTSMOUTH NH (USA)
SINGAPORE MADRID BOLOGNA ATHENS

British Library Cataloguing in Publication Data
Dyche, Roy
    Understanding and response. – (English in
    action)
    1. English language. Usage
    I. Title
    428

ISBN: 0 435 10227 3

Cover design: Design Revolution
Designed by Pen & Ink Book Company Ltd., Huntingdon, Cambridgeshire
Printed in Great Britain by Thomson Litho Ltd., East Kilbride, Scotland

Acknowledgements

The author is very grateful to Gail Swainston, Samantha Gibson, Cindy Ellis and Zoë Veitch for their advice and practical help in the preparation of this book.

The author and publishers would like to thank the following for permission to reproduce copyright material:

Alcohol Concern for extract from 'Your Body and Alcohol'; Animal Aid for 'Take Death Out of Your Diet'; BBC Radio for extract from 'You and Yours', BBC Radio 4, 21/6/89; Heather Buck for 'Moving House' by Heather Buck from *Interactions* (ed, Geoffrey Halson), Longman; Constable & Co Ltd for extracts from *The Generation Gap* by Mary McCormack; *The Daily Express* for 'Where Eagles Dare . . . 25/3/89'; *The Daily Mirror* for 'Skyride To Terror', 25/3/89; *The Daily Star* for 'Cops Club Dog to Death . . .' Faber & Faber Ltd for 'Rabbits' by Dorothy Nimmo from *First Fictions*; Margaret Franklin and Jan Creamer for extracts from article 'Animals In the Lab', *Woman's Own*, February 1988; Raymond Garlick for 'Thug' by Raymond Garlick from *Strictly Private*, ed. Roger McGough; *The Guardian* for 'A Woman Escapes by Rope . . .'; The Home Office for 'Safety Tips for Teenagers' and for statistics from Amusement Machines, HMSO Books and for graph 'Your Body and Alcohol from *Young People in 1986*; ISDD 2 (Institute for Study of Drug Dependance) for extract from *Drug Abuse Briefing*; Intasun Holidays for extract from Intasun brochure; IPC Magazines for extract from *Girl* Magazine; Methuen Children's Books for extract from *Goodbye Summer* by Alison Prince; Michael Joseph Ltd for 'The Little Palace' from *The Desperadoes* by Stan Barstow; Gareth Owen for 'My Sister Betty' by Gareth Owen from *Families Two*; Orlando Paterson for 'The Visitor' by Orlando Paterson; Random Century Group for 'The Lake' by Roger McGough from *Strictly Private*, and for 'The Wasteland' by Alan Paton from *Debbie Go Home*, Jonathan Cape, and for 'Remote' from *The Great Profundo and Other Stories*, Jonathan Cape; Reader's Digest Association Ltd for 'The Loch's Elusive Monster' from *Strange Stories, Amazing Facts*; Willy Russell for extract from *Educating Rita*; Shelter for extract from 'One Day I'll Have My Own Place to Stay'; Skytours for extract from Skytours brochure; Leslie Thomas for extract from *In My Wildest Dreams*; Which? magazine for 'Talking Shop', Which? August 1989.

We would like to thank the following for permission to reproduce photographs on the pages noted:

J. Allan Cash Ltd pp 13, 39, 48, 95; EMPICS pp 16, 18; Fortean Picture Library pp 51, 53; Sally and Richard Greenhill p 58; Topham Picture Source pp 24, 50, 58 (bottom); Andrew Wiard pp 106, 111; Which? magazine pp 28–31.

Contents

Introduction

The primary aim of this book, as its title suggests, is to help pupils develop the understanding and response skills demanded by both present GCSE syllabuses and the National Curriculum at key stage four. That is to say, the book is concerned most directly with National Curriculum attainment target 2: *The development of the ability to read, understand and respond to all types of writing.*

The reading matter has been chosen very carefully to reflect the variety of literary and non-literary material envisaged by the National Curriculum, and to be accessible and yet sufficiently demanding across the ability range. The assignments are designed to 'discriminate on a positive basis': it should be possible for every pupil to write something useful in answer to every question.

The **Understanding** sections invite them to explore the meaning and formal features of the passages in a straightforward way but one which allows abler pupils to display a grasp of what is implied rather than stated.

The **Response** exercises are of several sorts. Some ask pupils to formulate their own reasoned opinions on what they have read or to react to it in a persona different from their own. Others require them to assimilate information from the passage and re-present it in a different form, perhaps slanting their writing to express a given point of view. Others call for the more creative development of the material.

It is not expected that pupils will be asked to tackle all the questions on offer. Teachers will want to select those that best serve the needs of their particular groups and approximate most closely to the form of assessment for which they are preparing them.

However, the scope of the book extends beyond the Reading objectives of the National Curriculum and clearly both the Understanding and the Response assignments relate to attainment target 3: *A growing ability to construct and convey meaning in written language matching style to audience.*

The letters, reports, articles, campaign leaflets, advertisements and so forth that feature in the Response sections are especially important here, since, at several levels, the Writing target tells us that: *Pupils should be able to write in a variety of forms for a range of purposes, presenting subject matter differently to suit the needs of specified known audiences.*

Attainment target 3 is addressed also in the third section of exercises – **Your writing** – which encourages pupils to develop more freely the themes and ideas encountered in the reading matter, through their own stories, poems, description, discussion, and argument. Work of this sort, together with the more directed, instrumental Response writing, should find its way into GCSE coursework folders, as well as providing practice for the exams of boards that set similar tasks.

A short **Reference Section** at the end of the book offers pupils guidance on writing of different kinds, largely in the form of annotated examples.

In addition, the book affords considerable opportunity for oral work and the attainment of National Curriculum target 1: *The development of pupils' understanding of the spoken word and the capacity to express themselves effectively in* a variety of speaking and listening activities, matching style and response to audience and purpose.

Exercises in all three groups may be seen as occasions for class or small group discussion, and teachers should be aware of the many possibilities for role-play presented especially by the Response assignments. Those that may obviously be used in this way are indicated by the symbol though some simple change in wording may be necessary; for example, a question that requires pupils to write a letter to a friend will need to be redefined as role-play in pairs.

The work proposed relates closely, therefore, to the Reading, Writing and Speaking and Listening attainment targets of the National Curriculum. The remaining targets, which concern spelling, handwriting and the attractive and appropriate presentation of work, will, of course, be addressed whenever pupils attempt the exercises in writing – and most interestingly, when they are asked to produce leaflets, advertisements, newspaper articles and statistics.

It is not claimed that a book of this nature can possibly provide complete coverage of the new syllabus, but teachers may feel confident that many of the syllabus's most important objectives are at the centre of these assignments.

A note on the marking of the Understanding and Response exercises

Although at the time of writing very little is known about how our pupils' work is to be assessed at key stage four, it is reasonable to expect it will be done on the basis of *levels of response* – as is now the case with GCSE. We may assume that rather than a pupil's answer being marked on the number of points it contains, an assessment will be made of the quality of the pupil's response as defined in the Curriculum's statements of attainment and embodied in the assessment criteria of individual boards.

One implication of this approach is that an answer need not be long or exhaust all relevant material in order to display an impressive level of response and therefore score highly.

For this reason we decided not to follow the practice adopted by most GCSE boards of indicating in brackets after each question the maximum number of marks an answer can score. Doubtless in an examination such information helps candidates organise their time sensibly; the danger, however, is that they will suppose that the question with the highest tariff must be answered at the greatest length. The quality of the response is the thing, not the number of points paraphrased.

1

BETTER SAFE THAN SORRY

This advice leaflet was prepared by the police. Its aim is to get young people to protect themselves against violent crime.

SAFETY TIPS FOR TEENAGERS

Teenage girls in particular, but boys as well, can find themselves at risk, whether working at a part-time job or out in the evening. So you should try to follow these basic guidelines:

- Be sure your parents always know where you are and how to contact you.

- If possible, go out accompanied by friends and return home with them.

- If you do go out alone, arrange transport to and from where you are going – with a relative, friend or taxi – and confirm arrangements for your return journey before you set off.

- If your arranged transport from a concert or other event fails to arrive and you can see that you will be left on your own, speak to the organisers and ask to use their telephone to make arrangements. Ask to stay until transport arrives.

- Don't accept the offer of a lift from someone you've only just met.

- Try to find casual jobs, such as babysitting, through family or friends, and be careful about answering advertisements. Try to go with a parent or friend on the first day.

- When working a paper round, if strangers invite you into their homes or offer you a lift, politely refuse and move on quickly.

- Wherever you are, be aware of how to make an emergency telephone call and the quickest way out.

The reason people are so anxious about the level of violence in our society can be found in figures like the ones below. These are annual figures which refer to offences recorded by the police in England and Wales.

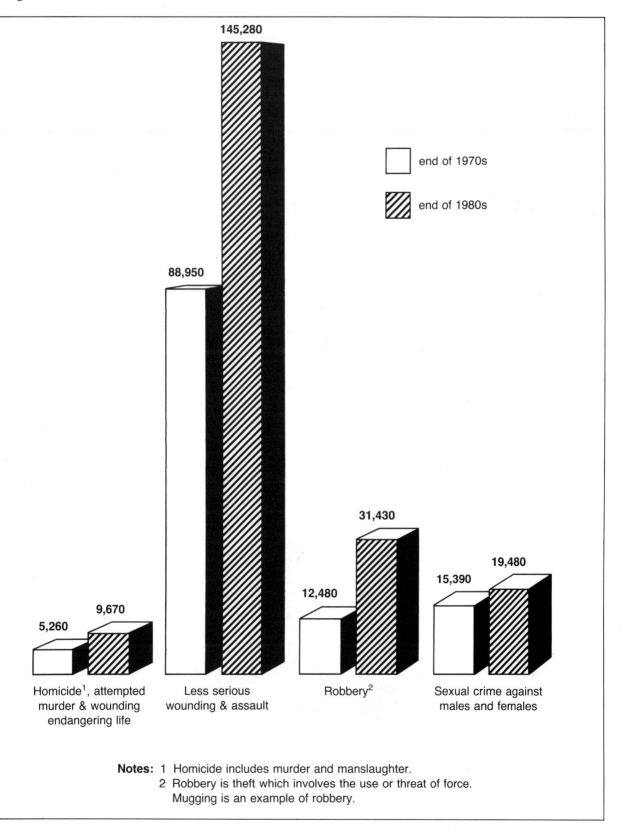

end of 1970s

end of 1980s

145,280

88,950

31,430

19,480

15,390

12,480

9,670

5,260

Homicide[1], attempted murder & wounding endangering life

Less serious wounding & assault

Robbery[2]

Sexual crime against males and females

Notes: 1 Homicide includes murder and manslaughter.
2 Robbery is theft which involves the use or threat of force.
Mugging is an example of robbery.

Understanding

1 According to the statistics on page 7:

Which of the four types of violent crime has more than doubled over the ten-year period?
Which has increased by the most cases?
Which has increased by the fewest cases?
Which is least likely to be committed in your area? Which is probably the most likely?

2 Sum up the statistics by writing two or three sentences which explain why most people will think they give a worrying picture of what is happening in our society.

3 All the advice in the leaflet on page 6 is very sensible but if you had to choose two or three of the recommendations as being especially important, which would they be? Why have you chosen these?

4 People often ignore perfectly good advice for fear of embarrassing themselves or others, or because it is a nuisance to do so. Which pieces of advice on page 6 might cause embarrassment or be inconvenient to follow? Give reasons for your answer.

5 Of course, the police want as many young people as possible to read the leaflet and understand it. How does the way it is designed and worded help to get the message across?

Response

Answer one of the following:

1 The leaflet on page 6 is part of a police drive to make teenagers more safety-conscious. To publicise the campaign, a police officer is interviewed on a radio or television news programme. In reply to the interviewer's questions, the officer discusses briefly the rise in violent crime, explains why there is special concern for young people and gives examples of the sort of advice being offered.

   Write the script of the interview. You should try to make the dialogue sound natural and unrehearsed, so do not simply copy out long passages from the leaflet or reel off a mass of complicated statistics. The suggestions on pages 124 and 125 will help you set out your work clearly.

2 A young teenager wants to go out for the evening to a disco but the parents are reluctant to agree. They have read the material on pages 6 and 7 and are not sure their son or daughter fully understands the risks or has made safe arrangements.

How might the conversation go? You may write this as a short story or set it out as a play after reading the suggestions on pages 124 and 125.

Answer one of the following:

1   Suppose someone your age ignores the advice in the leaflet on page 6 and, as a result, a situation develops which could easily have ended in disaster. Use this idea in a story that readers will find exciting but which will also act as a warning to them.

2   Primary children are at special risk from violent crime on their way to and from school. Design a leaflet that will help the older ones in this age group to understand the dangers and how to guard against them.
    Before you start on the leaflet, you need to decide the answers to certain questions, perhaps working in groups or pairs:
    What sort of advice is going to be most useful to these children?
    It is easy to upset youngsters, so how detailed should you be about what can happen to them if they ignore your advice?
    How ought you to set out, illustrate and word your leaflet if you are going to get through to people this age?

3   According to the figures on page 7, violence is on the increase in this country, but do you personally get the impression that you are living in a violent society? If so, can you think of reasons why more people are turning to violent crime these days and suggest some solutions to the problem?

2 So much for ROMANCE

I met her at evening classes. We began to talk about music and, in a moment of extravagance, I invited her to a concert at the Albert Hall. To my ecstasy and horror she accepted. She would telephone me to fix the day.

Now she did not know I was in an orphanage and I did not want her to know. This was when Mr Paul had become Superintendent and I was able to haunt the office on the Saturday, waiting for the phone to ring. It would never do for someone to pick it up and say: 'Dr Barnado's.' Fortunately she called at more or less the arranged time and I was swift to the receiver. I can still remember the number. 'Kingston 0232,' I responded in my poshest voice. Matron put her head in the door and went out again. 'Sorry,' I said and, to explain the pause, truthfully added: 'It was just one of the staff.' Now she thought we had servants too.

The meeting was arranged. She rang off, saying thrillingly that she was looking forward to seeing me again. Now I had the problem of obtaining money. As a senior boy I was getting half-a-crown a week pocket money and I worked out I could just manage the train fare and the lowest-priced tickets for a total of ten shillings. The sporting Mr Paul advanced me a month's pocket money on account of some fiction I related. On the day, shaking and shining, I went up to London on the train and then by bus to the Albert Hall. *There she was.* Waiting – for *me!* As though I took women out every night, I kissed her on the cheek.

Difficulties then began. She grumbled that we had to go and sit up in the highest *gods**, clumping and complaining up the endless stairs. When Cedric had taken her, she moaned, they had sat in the *front* stalls, just behind the conductor.

'You don't hear the music properly down there,' I argued with inspiration. We sat down. It was like peering into the mouth of a volcano. 'Up here the music floats to you.'

She kept muttering through the first half of the concert and then horrified me in the interval by announcing that she really *would* like a drink. Dumbstruck, I mentally counted the money in my pocket. 'Please, dear,' she said archly. 'A gin and ton.'

A gin and ton! Christ, how much was a gin and ton? Trembling, I went towards the bar. 'And *might* we have a programme?' she called after me. 'We ought to have bought the programme before *surely.*'

Sod the programme, I thought. But there was no escaping the gin and ton. I approached the bar; I had never bought a drink in my life. 'Gin and ton, please,' I mumbled.

The lady had a suspicious eye and I had a sudden hope that she would refuse to serve me. It would, on the other hand, be a humiliation to admit that I had been turned away as being under-age. But that gin and tonic would mean that I would not have enough to buy her ticket on the train home. I gritted my teeth while the bar lady hesitated.

* The gods: the cheapest seats in a theatre or concert hall, furthest from the stage and very high up.

She made up her mind and said: 'All right then. How many? Two?'

'*One!*' I bellowed. She fell back shocked. 'One, please, just one,' I whispered.

It left me with only enough money for the bus fare to Waterloo and my own return ticket. I would have to give her that. Jesus Christ, a gin and ton, if you please!

'Aren't you having one?' inquired the girl loftily when I returned.

'Me? Oh no. I'm in training, see. For football, I've had to cut out drink. Especially gin and ton.'

She sniffed. 'Did you get a programme? I'd like to know what they're playing even if we are a long way up.'

'Sold out,' I said desperately. 'All gone. Anyway I think it's more fun guessing, don't you?'

'Not really,' she said. 'I feel quite giddy up here you know.'

★　★　★

I was glad when it was over. We silently boarded the bus and she stared out of the window all the way to Waterloo. She took out a gold case and selected a cigarette which I tremblingly lit for her with her own box of Swan Vestas. I was so miserable.

At the station I felt for my return ticket and prepared to hand it to her, planning to announce at the same time that, although it was eleven-thirty at night, I had remembered a sudden urgent appointment in the City. To my overwhelming relief she produced a season-ticket from her bag. I wouldn't have to walk after all.

At the other end she gave me a peck like a hen on the cheek before heading for home. So much for romance. I brightened when I was walking up Gloucester Road, though. I woke my friend Nightshirt and told him how wonderful it had all been, the Albert Hall, the inspiring music, the gin and tonics. He stirred in the dormitory moonlight. 'That must have set you back a packet,' he mentioned.

'Oh, it did,' I said, getting into my iron bed. 'But it was worth it. She's terrific.'

Nightshirt sniffed over the blankets. 'That's the trouble with women,' he said wisely. 'It's the bloody expense.'

LESLIE THOMAS
In My Wildest Dreams

Boys Boys Boys

you can understand them (almost)

You don't need a degree in psychology to understand the opposite sex, although sometimes it might feel like it. They're just like us really, but a LOT stranger.

HE SEEMED SO KEEN

Q "I've lost count of the number of times I've met a boy at a party and he's taken my phone number, but never called. And they seem so keen at the time."

A Unfortunately, this is completely and utterly normal. It may be that the guy concerned really does mean to phone, but changes his mind later. Or he may just be saying "goodbye it was nice knowing you. I haven't the guts to walk away without asking for your phone number and giving you all sorts of false hopes."

HE IGNORES ME

Q "Jack and I get on really well. We often go out together and have a lot of laughs. The trouble is, when his mates are around he either ignores me completely or makes nasty remarks about me. Why does he do it?"

A Basically, to try and look big. And if his mates have got the intelligence of an earthworm, that is what he will do. However, if they've got an ounce of savvy they'll only laugh and egg him on because that's what everyone else is doing. Although they may act all macho, most boys don't have a lot of confidence and this stupid laughing at girls stuff is just a phase. The truth is, he is happy to have you as his girlfriend and he does want to spend time with you. But he doesn't want his mates taking the mickey out of him, and if they're a bit jealous because they aren't going out with anyone, that's just what they're likely to do. It's pretty much the way they used to behave when they were seven, except that they've put their water pistols away.

We reckon the best thing you can do is disappear when his pals are around. He won't always behave this way, so just give him a chance to get on with it.

HE'S DRIVING ME CRAZY

Q "Stephen is really driving me crazy. We go out together for a few weeks and then I hear nothing from him for ages. I phone and he's not in, if I call round to his house he's always out. Then just when I'm about to give up hope, he rings to arrange a date and we're back to normal. He knows I hate him doing this, but he still does it. Why?"

A Because you let him. When you really like someone it's all too easy to let them walk all over you, girls do it all the time. But in the long run it doesn't get you very far. We've got a

nasty feeling that Stephen only sees you when he's got nothing else to do. Or, no other girl to see.

Next time he does this to you, don't sit at home moping, go out and have some fun with your friends. And when he gets round to ringing, tell him you've met someone else, even if it is an out and out lie. If you don't he'll carry on like this until he finds a girl he doesn't want to two-time and then you won't see him for dust. It hurts, but it's true.

TOO SCARED TO DATE

Q "Whenever there's a party or a disco on, Chris and I get off together. He's all over me, but he never asks me out. Why?"

A Because he doesn't want to. If he's got the confidence to smooch you all the way round the dance floor, he'd be able to pluck up the courage to ask for a date if he wanted one.

You have to accept that this is as far as things will go between you and Chris. As long as it suits you, that's fine. If it doesn't, next time he puckers up, tell him to pucker off!

taken from *GIRL* magazine

Understanding

1 What evidence is there in the story that this is probably the first time Leslie has taken a girl out on a proper date?

2 It is mainly Leslie Thomas's descriptions of the different emotions and feelings he had during this episode that make the story amusing. Choose three or four places where Leslie's feelings come over strongly, say what these feelings are and explain why the boy has them.

3 Most readers will not find the girl very likable. What does she say and do during the evening that gives us a poor impression of her?

4 What picture does the *Girl* article paint of the average boy? Describe the attitudes he is supposed to have according to the magazine.

5 How well does this picture of boys apply to Leslie? Does anything said in the article fit the way he thinks and behaves in the story, or is he completely different from the magazine's 'typical boy'?

Response

Answer one of the following:

1 Leslie is obviously very anxious to impress the girl, despite the great difficulties he faces before and during the date. Referring closely to details in the story, say how well you think he copes with these difficulties.

2 Imagine the girl in the story writes to a friend about her evening with Leslie.

Bearing in mind what we gather from the passage about her attitudes and her opinions of Leslie, write the letter you think she might have sent. Read the suggestions on page 122 before you begin.

3 How do you react to the *Girl* article? It says it is helping its readers to understand boys' behaviour, but, in your experience, is it presenting a false 'stereotyped' view of boys or are most of them really the way *Girl* describes them? Refer closely to some of the ideas in the article and give clear reasons for your own views.

Your writing

Answer one of the following:

1 Earlier in the book from which the story is taken, Leslie Thomas says: 'I was very romantic, and still am, about women.' Unfortunately this particular occasion hardly lives up to his romantic expectations.

Either write a different, shorter version of the same evening, starting as Leslie gets off the bus at the Albert Hall; or describe another of his dates. Whichever you choose, let the outing be a success by making his partner a much more suitable girl.

2 Write a true or imagined story about a time when, like Leslie or the girls in the article, your high hopes were disappointed.

You could write about a disco, party, trip or holiday, about starting a club or a new school, meeting or going out with someone you always admired, or any other occasion that was a big let-down.

3 This is one person's opinion of magazines for teenage girls:

They do enormous harm by brainwashing their readers into a ridiculously narrow view of life – the view that being a girl is all about make-up, fashion, pop music and, above all, boys. Their ideal girl spends hours in front of her mirror and is cunning enough to get herself a boy her friends will envy – preferably one who looks like the latest pop idol.

Is this how you see these magazines? Explain your views clearly and, if possible, back up your points with examples.

3
ALL
ABOARD
FOR THE
SKYLARK!

A WOMAN escapes by rope from a cable car stranded over a 100-ft ravine at the Alton Towers leisure complex in Staffordshire yesterday.

She was among 28 people rescued from three cars after the one in which she was riding became tangled with a communications cable in high winds. A computerised safety system halted the 40-car Sky Ride, leaving some passengers trapped for more than two hours.

The emergency services practised just such a rescue at Alton Towers two weeks ago, with staff acting as trapped passengers.

A wheelchair-bound man stranded more than an hour in the car left hanging over the ravine was lowered to safety by firemen, who dropped a rope to the ground below after getting to the car with special equipment.

Other passengers were rescued with a hydraulic platform and turntable ladders.

PHOTOGRAPH: PHIL O'BRIEN

from *The Guardian*

SKYRIDE TO TERROR

TEARS: A mother breaks down as she is reunited with her son

Cable car traps trippers

THE thrill of the fair turned to horror for 27 Easter trippers on an Alpine-style skyride yesterday.

Terrified passengers were stranded in mid-air above a 100ft ravine for an agonising two hours after their cable cars shuddered to a halt at Britain's biggest amusement park.

A small child who clung desperately to his rescuer was among the frightened holidaymakers who had to be lowered to safety by ropes in a near-gale.

His relieved mother broke down in tears as they were reunited in the ambulance taking them from

By FRANK CORLESS

Alton Towers, Staffordshire.

Rescue hero Mark Symonds had to inch his way along the cable on pulleys to reach the cars.

Stranded

He battled with the high winds to climb down a ladder into the stranded cable car.

Mark, 25, said afterwards: "The people inside were obviously very relieved to see me."

One weeping girl said: "I thought we'd never get down. I kept thinking 'We're going to die.'"

Fire chief Peter Hollands said: "Rescue attempts were made more difficult by the high winds and the difficult terrain."

SAVED: A young mum

from the *Daily Mirror*

Where Eagles Dare rescue at 100ft

AT LEAST 28 holiday-makers were trapped 100ft up when a leisure park cable car ride ground to a halt yesterday in high winds.

For nearly four hours, one gondola stuck in a tangled wire was buffeted as it hung above a tree-lined ravine on the multi-million pound Skyride at Alton Towers in Staffordshire.

Passengers joked and sang to keep up their spirits.

And they were finally rescued in a scene straight out of Alastair Maclean's Where Eagles Dare.

A three-man rescue team, led by modest hero Mark Symonds, 25, climbed out on to the support

By MIKE ATCHINSON, TOBY McDONALD and PHILIP DERBYSHIRE

cable, hooked a sling on it, swung themselves out into mid-air and slid down to the car.

They dropped on to the roof, and climbed in by a ladder attached to the outside.

The passengers were all given safety harnesses to wear, then lowered by rope to safety below.

Some passengers managed to climb down from other gondolas, but three, including the one which was tangled, were too high up.

Firemen using hydraulic lifts brought down 10 people from the first car, three at a time, and six from the second, but the last gondola was out of the longest lift's reach.

One of those rescued, six-year-old Andrew Rowbottom, joked: "Coming down the rope was the best ride there.

But mother-of-three Deborah Ward refused to let her four-year-old son Westley slide down on his own. Instead he was strapped to rescuer Stephen Maddock's back as his mother prayed as he slid down.

Rescue team leader Mark said: "It was all quite straightforward. When you practise it every week, which we do as a routine measure, then there's no real problem involved."

Mark: Leader

Stranded: One of the cable cars

from the *Daily Express*

1 Piece together information from the three articles and explain clearly in your own words why the cable cars stopped and how the rescue of passengers in the various cars was carried out.

2 It is hard to know exactly what happened at Alton Towers that day because there are some puzzling differences between the three newspaper reports — for example, we cannot be sure how many people had to be rescued: 27? 28? more than 28? What other differences of this sort can you find?

3 Decide which of the articles gets the most drama and excitement out of the story, then explain how this has been done. You should look at the particular facts the article stresses — and perhaps exaggerates — and at the words used to describe these facts.

Answer one of the following:

1 An inquiry is ordered into the incident described in the newspaper articles, to discover what caused it and how well the rescue was handled. The police collect written statements from several of those involved, asking them to be as unemotional as they can and to keep to the facts they know first-hand.

   Basing your work on what you have learned from the articles, write the statements that might be provided by the mother of the child mentioned in the second article and by Mark Symonds, the leader of the rescue team.

2 Imagine that the events at Alton Towers are reported on the television news that evening. The newsreader briefly outlines the story and then a reporter gives a more detailed account whilst viewers are shown videofilm of the scene. The items ends with two or three short interviews conducted soon after the rescue with people referred to in the newspaper articles.

   Write the full script from the newsreader's introduction onwards, deciding for yourself which people should be interviewed. The example on page 125 will help you set out your work in the right way.

3 Give an account of what occurred at Alton Towers as it might appear in the diary of somebody who was trapped in one of the cable cars. Take the basic facts from the newspaper articles but fill them out with details of your own. Aim to give the impression of a really dramatic incident that produced powerful feelings in you.

Your writing

Answer one of the following:

1 Write a piece of description, a poem if you wish, set in a fairground or leisure park. Select your details carefully so that they build up a strong picture of the fun, excitement and bustle of the place.

2 Tell a true or imaginary story which ends with a thrilling rescue. You could choose, for example, a rescue at sea, or from being trapped underground, on a cliff or in a fire.

   You should aim to involve the reader by creating suspense, so think about how writers and film-makers do this. For instance, they may slow down the action at key points, so we feel we are living through the events ourselves.

3 Take some incident, if possible one you actually witnessed or were involved in, for example, a road accident, a fire or a street brawl, and write two different newspaper reports of it. Make the first quite a short, low-key account which might appear on an inside page of a 'quality' paper like 'The Guardian'. The second should be a much more sensational version that could make the front page of a 'popular' paper like the 'Daily Mirror'.

   Even if the happening itself was nothing very special, your second article should inject as much drama into it as possible. If you study and discuss the articles on pages 16 to 18, you will see some of the techniques reporters use to excite their readers. You should also read the suggestions on page 121.

Rabbits

They were in the orchard, under the apple trees, making tea-parties in the summer house. The little table was laid out with a tea-cloth; they had put buttercups in an egg cup and made brown bread and butter for a real tea-party. An uncle had given them each a china rabbit; the two rabbits were going to have tea. Kate's rabbit was blue, its features only lightly indented, its ears lying along its back in a smooth curve. Ellen's was a more realistic rabbit, the fur suggested by a slight roughness in the clay. The two rabbits sat side by side on the table.

'Oh I do love my rabbit,' said Kate, elder by two years. 'He is so smooth and shiny and such a beautiful blue. Come along, Rabbit, would you like some bread and butter, or would you rather have a buttercup for your tea?'

'I like my rabbit better,' said Ellen determinedly. She was a square child who fell over continually; her skinned knees never healed properly, so that she went through the summer patched with elastoplast. She admired Kate because Kate was older and braver and knew much more than she did. Kate was lovable and talkative and naughty and pretty and Kate was older.

'I like my rabbit better. Really,' said Ellen.

'Do you?' said Kate. 'He's awfully ordinary, just brown and rabbity. Mine is blue. Blue like the sea, blue like the sky and he's smooth, like those pebbles you get on the beach.'

Ellen was increasingly aware of the extraordinary charm of Kate's rabbit. Her own rabbit looked more and more ordinary, boringly realistic. She was thoughtful.

She said, 'I think your rabbit is lovely, Kate. I think your rabbit is much nicer than mine. Oh, Kate, it isn't fair! I wish Uncle Tom had given me one like yours. I want a rabbit like yours!'

'All right,' said Kate carelessly, 'I don't mind. You can have mine and I'll have yours.'

Ellen could hardly believe she had got her own way so easily. She suspected there must be a snag. But Kate smiled and held out the beautiful smooth-eared rabbit. Ellen took him. Kate got some biscuits out of the tin they had brought up the garden. They drank their orange juice out of the dolls' teacups with the strange taste from the not quite clean bottoms of the cups, and then they started to weed between the cracks of the summer-house terrace. The rabbits sat beside them.

'Oh, I do love my new rabbit,' said Kate, scraping away with a kitchen knife. 'Mind you get the roots out, Elly, they'll only grow again if you don't.'

'They'll grow again anyway, they always do,' said Ellen.

'Of course they grow again in the end, but if you don't get the roots out we might as well not be doing this job at all. Go down and get a brush, will you?'

Ellen went down the garden path to the shed. She picked a bunch of redcurrants from the bush and burst them, one by one, in her mouth, juicy and sour.

'I see you!' shouted Kate. 'You're eating redcurrants and there won't be any left for jelly. I'll tell. Mum thinks it's the birds, but it's you, you eat them all the time. No wonder you're fat!'

'I'm not fat. Redcurrants aren't fattening and, anyway, I'm not fat!'

But Ellen was in despair because she knew she was fat. When she got back with the brush, Kate had stopped weeding and was making her rabbit climb the cherry tree.

'Do you know why I love my rabbit?' said Kate. 'It's because he is so brown, and I love the way his nose looks real. I love the way his ears go along his back like a real rabbit and the little rough bits he has on his fur. I might call him Rough.'

'I'm going to call mine Blue,' said Ellen.

'That's a funny name for a rabbit!'

'Rough is a dog's name anyway.'

'Look,' said Kate. 'If I hide him in the grass a bit and cover him with this bit of meadowsweet, it makes a house for him. He's just coming out to eat his dinner. Look, he looks as if he lives in this little hole!'

'I'm going to make a house for my rabbit,' said Ellen.

'Oh, no that's no good,' said Kate. 'Your rabbit is so blue! You can see he isn't a real rabbit. He's the wrong colour for a garden rabbit, he's no good outside. You'll have to keep him on your dressing-table for an ornament. I think I'll leave my rabbit out all night to live in this hole and in the morning maybe he'll have turned into a real rabbit and run away with all the other rabbits to live with them!'

'He'll get myxi!' said Ellen.*

'Oh, don't be mean, Elly, of course he won't. If you left your rabbit out, all the others would mob him, like birds do owls in the daytime, you know because he'd be the wrong colour. Anyway, he hasn't got proper legs!'

Ellen fought with herself but she could not resist the pictures Kate put into her mind.

'Oh, Kate, I wish I hadn't given you my rabbit! It was mine in the first place, because Uncle Tom gave him to me. I've changed my mind, he's much the nicest rabbit and Uncle Tom meant me to have him, so he's mine really!'

Kate smiled, conscious of her power.

'All right,' she said. 'You can have your rabbit back if you like. I don't mind. If you're going to make a fuss.'

Ellen took the brown rabbit. She made a nest by the corner of the summer-house steps and lined it with leaves. She decorated it with cranesbill and buttercups and laid her rabbit in the nest. And it did look almost real.

But Kate smoothed her hand over the blue rabbit and a smile turned up the corners of her mouth. She said, softly crooning, thoughtful, 'I do love my blue rabbit and Uncle Tom meant me to have him because he's special. He is smooth and shiny and blue like the sea. I could take him to Jenny Brown's Point and put him in the sea and the waves would wash over him. He'd go all lovely colours like the pebbles do and I expect he can swim, too. He's a sea-rabbit.'

'There's no such thing,' said Ellen.

'Yes, there is. There's sea-horses and sea-urchins and sea-dogs, so there is sea-rabbits and mine is. Mine is the best rabbit in the world!'

And it was the truth, and Ellen recognised it.

DOROTHY NIMMO

*Ellen is referring to myxomatosis, an extremely unpleasant disease in rabbits.

My Sister Betty

My sister Betty said,
'I'm going to be a famous actress.'
Last year she was going to be a missionary.
'Famous actresses always look unhappy but beautiful,'
She said pulling her mouth sideways
And making her eyes turn upwards
So they were mostly white.
'Do I look unhappy but beautiful?'
'I want to go to bed and read,' I said.
'Famous actresses suffer and have hysterics,' she said.
'I've been practising my hysterics.'
She began going very red and screaming
So that it hurt my ears.
She hit herself on the head with her fists
And rolled off my bed onto the lino.
I stood by the wardrobe where it was safer.
She got up saying, 'Thank you, thank you,'
And bowed to the four corners of my bedroom.
'Would you like an encore of hysterics?' she asked.
'No,' I said from inside the wardrobe.
There was fluff all over her vest.
'If you don't clap enthusiastically,' she said,
'I'll put your light out when you're reading.'
While I clapped a bit
She bowed and shouted, 'More, more.'
My mother shouted upstairs,
'Go to bed and stop teasing, Betty.'
'The best thing about being a famous actress,' Betty said,
'Is that you die a lot.'
She fell to the floor with a crash
And lay there for an hour and a half
With her eyes staring at the ceiling.
She only went away when I said,
'You really look like a famous actress.'
When I got into bed and started reading
She came and switched off my light.
It's not much fun
Having a famous actress for a sister.

GARETH OWEN

Understanding

1 We are not told the ages of the two girls in *Rabbits.* What information in the story helps us to decide roughly how old they are?

2 Can you explain why Kate seems to find it so easy to get her sister to swap rabbits? Has it anything to do with the personalities of the two girls?

3 Kate ends up with the blue rabbit, the one she had in the first place. So what was the point of it all? Does the story suggest to you any reason for Kate's behaviour?

4 In Gareth Owen's poem, what is it that appeals to Betty about being a famous actress? Does your answer tell us anything about the sort of girl Betty is?

5 The poet wants us to find the whole incident funny. What details in the poem are there to amuse us?

Response

Answer one of the following:

1 Ellen in *Rabbits* and the boy in the poem are both given a hard time by their sisters. For which of the two 'victims' do you have more sympathy? Look closely at how they are treated and give clear reasons for your answer.

2 Imagine that Kate's mother is getting worried about the way Kate treats her sister, and that Betty's mother is just as concerned about her daughter's behaviour. Both parents decide to write to the problems page of *Home,* a magazine that aims to give practical advice on matters like these.

   Write the two letters the mothers send to the magazine. In each case, explain clearly what is causing concern, briefly describing the incident in the story or the poem and perhaps mentioning one or two similar incidents. Follow each letter with the sort of good advice you think the magazine might offer.

   Read pages 122 and 123 before you begin, and treat these as formal letters.

Your writing

Answer one of the following:

1 Write about the games you used to play as a child, either alone or with other children, especially games involving the sort of make-believe we see in the story and the poem.

2 Sometimes a relationship like Kate and Ellen's continues right into adulthood, with one person dominating the other; sometimes the victim manages to break free and lead his or her own life.

Write a follow-up to *Rabbit*, imagining the girls are now your age or older. Has anything changed in their relationship?

3   Gareth Owen writes:

> *My sister Betty said,*
> *'I'm going to be a famous actress.'*
> *Last year she was going to be a missionary.*

Describe your own ambitions, both those you had when you were younger, which perhaps make you smile now, and those you have at present.

5
TALKING SHOP

This is part of a report published in the consumer magazine *Which?* :

Ever entered a store and come away with more than you intended to buy? We reveal the selling devices shops use that are designed to make you spend, spend, spend.

Retailers, big and small, are obviously in business to make a profit. To achieve this, they need to ring up sales. And to do this, they have to satisfy their customers' 'needs' as well as play upon their 'wants'. Providing choice and quality, convenience, competitive prices and so forth are all vital to a store if it is to attract customers back again and again.

Retailers may go to great lengths, too, to create a pleasant shopping environment to encourage shoppers to linger. In doing this, they've managed to turn much of our shopping into a major leisure activity — a 1987 special report by Mintel on British Lifestyles found that more than a third of people not only enjoy shopping but also the shopping environment itself.

But, in the fiercely competitive world of retailing, that's not the whole story behind shopping psychology. Many shoppers, it seems, enter stores not knowing what they intend to buy. According to a recent study on buying behaviour conducted by Marketing Sciences, some 58 per cent of supermarket shoppers decided what to buy only when they got in a store — of those, well over half bought on impulse. So there's plenty of scope for retailers to influence what we spend.

Some selling techniques are obvious enough — for example, sales promotions such as back-of-pack offers and point-of-sale leaflets. Others are less apparent. For this report, we reveal some of the ingenious ways supermarkets and chainstores strive to influence your shopping.

Of course, customers benefit from some of these sales techniques. However, it's worth being aware of them. It might help you resist temptation the next time you embark on a shopping trip, or at least inject some fun into the weekly grocery shop to see how many you can spot in your local store.

The image of freshness

Supermarkets know from their market research that shoppers place a premium on fresh produce

being in stores. They may place their fruit and veg at the entrance of a store, or even a display of house plants for sale, to enhance this. They may also provide an in-store bakery that wafts irresistible fresh bread smells around a large area of the store. The colour of the store's fixtures may heighten the image, too — for example, green may be used because of its association with fresh produce. The bulk of what supermarkets sell — pre-packaged grocery items such as frozen foods and washing powders — may in fact be quite different from this image.

Layout — picking the place

The location of products in the store is considered all-important in determining how well a particular brand sells. Nowhere is this more developed than in supermarkets. With computerised stock-control, supermarkets can find out where in a store shoppers will select items from the most. In these areas can be found products with the highest mark-ups or ones which, though less profitable, sell very quickly.

Traditionally in retailing, 'eye-level' means 'buy-level' — shelves at eye height are eagerly sought by manufacturers, or may be reserved for certain own-brand items. The so-called 'gondola ends' (shelves that face the middle aisles and the checkouts) are also sought-after areas. Increasingly popular is 'complementation' — placing dessert or salad dressings, say, over units containing ice cream or items that may be eaten with salads such as burgers.

Chocs near the checkout

A common ploy is for supermarkets to place chocs and the like near the checkout. Their location may help reduce theft but it's a successful selling technique as well: parents are sorely tempted to buy them to pacify bored children while the weekly shop is being rung up. It's a practice that supermarkets are increasingly criticised for, and one which some of them have dropped.

Spreading staples

Supermarkets may spread low-price staples such as bread, tea and sugar, around their stores, and a long way from the entrance — shoppers have to pass tempting higher-profit lines on the way. In similar vein, chainstores may locate the products they have a good reputation for as far away from the store entrance as possible. They can rely on a degree of customer loyalty towards these products, so they gamble that shoppers will go actively looking for them around the store, passing other wares which might tempt them.

Shifting products around the store

Shoppers may know their local supermarket layout intimately and time their weekly shop down to the last second. One of the spin-offs of shifting products around is that shoppers don't get into too much of a routine and by-pass other tempting goodies. Shifting products can be counter-productive, though, since shoppers may get annoyed when products are no longer where they used to be.

Lighting to effect

Both supermarkets and chainstores give careful thought to lighting. With chainstores, the aim is to achieve lighting which is as close to natural light as possible so that shoppers get a fair idea what the colour of clothes will be like in daylight. With supermarkets, special lighting (and mirrors) may be used to enhance certain foods, particularly fresh fruit and veg.

Floor layout leads you through

Many chainstores have divided up their floors with different carpeting — one pattern for the routes through a store and one defining sales areas. Shoppers are drawn naturally along these routes — known in the trade as the 'Yellow Brick Road'. It's a subtle device to get them deep into the store and in amongst the merchandise. But it's not always successful — some shoppers are reluctant to stray off the routes into the sales

areas. So Marks and Spencer, for example, use wood or marble covering for routes, encouraging shoppers to walk on the more welcoming carpet in sales areas.

In-store advertising

As you enter a supermarket, giant colour photographs of succulent roasts, fancy cakes and cheeses hit you — irresistible if you've had nothing to eat before setting out on your shopping trip. In the United States, 'video trolleys' are being tried out in a small number of supermarkets. Each trolley has a screen which advertises products as you shop. Sensors at the end of shelves trigger relevant advertising — so a shopper passing the cook-chill cabinets, say,

may receive an ad on the screen for ready-made moussaka. Such trolleys are aimed unashamedly at the impulse shopper, and the makers claim they increase sales by around 30 per cent.

The mega-trolley

The extra-large supermarket trolley — roughly a third bigger than a decade ago — is a welcome aid to convenience shopping, particularly if you do a big food shop only once or twice a month. Whatever the intention, there's a benefit to the supermarket, too, for the trolley goes on looking emptier longer, which may encourage you to buy more.

The sound of Muzak

Many retailers clearly regard piped-music as a sound selling device. The music, which may well be instrumental and played continuously, is specially arranged and recorded so that, unlike radio, say, it is not intrusive — it's designed to be heard but not listened to.

So does it really work as a sales technique? The makers of piped-music claim that it does, of course. It's said to relax shoppers, making them less impatient and more likely to want to linger in a store.

Independent research in the United States suggests that the pace at which the shoppers move around may be influenced by the tempo of background music. The slower you move around a store, the more likely you are to buy, so slow tempo music is selected to encourage you to move more slowly. At one supermarket in the United States, where a detailed study was carried out, an increase of more than one-third in sales was recorded as a result of selecting slower tempo music.

Understanding

1 Why is background music in supermarkets supposed to increase sales?

2 If a particular profitable item was not selling well in a supermarket which of the techniques mentioned in the article might be used to tempt more customers to buy it?

3 Although stores are only really concerned to improve their profits, we are told that some of the methods *Which?* describes do, in fact, benefit the customer as well. List the ones you think do this and explain clearly how shoppers can be said to benefit from them.

Response

Answer one of the following:

1 Imagine that you run a small, old-fashioned grocery shop. You believe in 'honest', straightforward selling and strongly disapprove of the methods used in modern stores. Write your reactions to the *Which?* report, making it clear what in general you dislike about the techniques described there and explaining which ones you find especially unpleasant.

2 A consumer magazine receives the letter on the opposite page.
The magazine editor decides to publish Ms Warrilow's letter, and, beneath it, explain why stores do the things she complains of.

Basing your work on relevant parts of the *Which?* report, write the explanations the editor might give. Bear in mind that replies to readers' letters are normally written in a sympathetic, friendly way.

Your writing

Answer one of the following:

1 The report says shopping is now a 'major leisure activity' – an idea that would have seemed odd a few years ago. How important and enjoyable a part do shops play in *your* life? These are the sort of questions you might consider:

Apart from the pleasure of buying things you want, are there shops you just like being in for one reason or another? Do you get fun out of window-shopping with friends? If so, what would a typical outing be like? Do you enjoy the entertainment and other activities often found in shopping precincts these days?

2 A busy supermarket or chainstore provides plenty of material for descriptive writing: the colourful displays, the varied appearance and behaviour of customers and staff, and generally the bustling, noisy activity of the store. Try to capture all this in a word picture — a poem if you wish — packed with carefully described detail.

3 The *Which?* report seems to suggest that stores make us want things we do not really need. It is often claimed that we are now a 'consumer society', that we have been fooled into the idea that we cannot be truly happy unless we are buying luxuries we could easily do without.

   What are your own opinions on this question? Do you think we have somehow lost the knack of enjoying ourselves without spending money? Have we stopped believing 'the best things in life are free'?

```
Dear Editor,
        I wish supermarkets would think more  about their layouts.
For example, fruit and vegetables get spoilt at the bottom of a
trolley, so positioning this section at the entrance to the store
is bad planning. Also, cheaper items are often placed either too
high or too low on the shelves, and the basics tend to be
scattered all over the store rather than kept conveniently
together. It takes several visits before you learn where they all
are - then suddenly you're back to square one because, for no
good reason, they've taken it into their heads to rearrange the
shelves.
        Supermarket managers seem totally unaware of the importance
of layout, and I'm sure their sales must suffer as a result.

                        Yours faithfully,
                        Pam Warrilow
                        (Stoke-on-Trent)
```

6
An Awkward Customer

Mrs Marshall said, 'Don't just stand there, Miss Bowman — serve the customer.' And she stalked off.

'What a cow,' said Liz cheerfully. 'I better get out of your hair before you get the sack. See you tomorrow.'

Liz jumped off the bin and went out. I could see Mrs Marshall frowning at me from behind the cash register so I went over to see what the boy who had pushed past us wanted. He was turning over an Adidas trainer in his big, dirty hands, and I thought he looked as suspicious as a chimpanzee I saw once at the Zoo, inspecting an empty beer can. 'They got gold laces or something?' he asked. 'Hell of a price, isn't it?'

I said we'd got some other ones, and showed him. He wasn't too pleased with those either. 'Load of rubbish,' he said.

I could see he was going to be difficult. 'What about basketball boots?' I suggested. 'Lots of people buy those.'

He lounged against the rack and folded his arms. The yellow crash-helmet stuck out from his elbow, taking up a lot of room. His hair was dark and tousled and he looked bored. I thought he was a real hard case. 'Go on, then,' he said. 'Show me what you got.'

I very nearly told him to go and look for himself. The place was now crammed with other customers and Mrs Marshall was ringing up purchases like a robot gone mad. Poor old Mr Biggs was trying to sell sandals to a huge family complete with screaming baby. But Mrs Marshall glared at me again so I trotted round to the basketball boots like a good girl and came back with an armful. 'These are the most expensive ones, but they've got really good padding round the ankles,' I told him. 'Then there's these Union Jack ones, or the yellow and black —' I wondered why I was bothering. He wasn't going to buy any shoes. He was just idling some time away. I had done it so often myself that I could spot it a mile off.

'Might as well try something on,' he said, and he slumped down on a chair and flung his foot up on a footstool. He didn't make any attempt to undo the laces of his grubby plimsolls.

I said, 'What size do you take?'

He shrugged. 'Dunno.' I looked at him, trying to keep my temper. Under his leather jacket he wore a white shirt without a collar, unironed and crumpled, but a lovely quality poplin, the sort of thing I'd have bought if I'd seen it in a junk shop. And he had a red cotton scarf round his neck. He knew I was getting cross. He grinned and said, 'Aren't you going to measure my feet, then?' I took a measuring stick from under the footstool and tugged at the laces of his beastly plimsoll.

'They used to have those machines when I was a kid,' he said. 'You stood in a sort of hole and the sides slid in, front to back and side to side.' He demonstrated with his hands. 'Zerp — zerp. Then the numbers came up on a little video. Don't you have one of them?'

'No, we don't,' I snapped. 'You want a size eleven.'

'See what you can find, then, darling,' he said. He pulled a tin of tobacco and a packet of papers from his pocket and began to make himself a cigarette.

I came back with another armful of shoes. 'There's this one,' I said patiently, 'or this — but we've only got the Union Jack basketball boots in your size. Or you could have a pair of tennis shoes.'

He leaned back as if he was a Roman emperor and flicked ash on the carpet from his skinny cigarette. 'Wouldn't be seen dead in Union Jacks,' he said. 'And them Adidas is too much bread. I'll try the trainers.'

I said, 'You can try those on while I see to someone else, can't you? There's a lot of people waiting.'

He shook his head. 'Don't give me that, darling,' he said. 'Like a woman at the hairdresser's, innit? Come in for a bit of pampering. Spot of the old grovel. Got your little shoe horn, have you?'

Suddenly I blew up. I jumped to my feet, absolutely blazing with fury. 'I'm not grovelling to you or anyone else,' I shouted at him. 'You didn't come in here to buy any shoes, you came to muck me about. Well, you can just shove off and try it on someone else, because as far as I'm concerned, it's just *not on!*'

Everyone was staring. Mrs Marshall came rushing up and said, 'That is quite enough, Miss Bowman!' Mr Biggs was behind her, looking more flustered than ever. 'What on earth is going on?' he asked.

It was Mrs Marshall's moment of triumph. She raised her thin eyebrows at him and said, 'I think you will agree, Mr Biggs, that Miss Bowman's trial period has *not* been satisfactory!' And she stalked off to the cash desk. I had played right into her hands. I was so angry that I almost wept. 'I don't care,' I said obstinately. 'There's some things I just won't put up with.'

The boy had put both feet on the footstool. He was sitting back comfortably with his arms folded and his ankles crossed, and his cigarette stuck out of his mouth at a jaunty angle. He was

thoroughly enjoying the scene he had caused. 'That woman's a right old bat,' he told Mr Biggs conversationally, jerking his head in the direction of Mrs Marshall. 'You want to get rid of her, to start with.' He grinned and added, 'This popsy with the candyfloss hair's all right. Just wants to learn a bit of proper respect, that's all.' I looked at him with hatred. He wiggled the toes of his shoeless foot luxuriously. There was a large hole in his sock.

I wanted to keep my job. I knew I had been amazingly lucky to get it, and in any case, the thought of telling Mum I'd got the sack was a nightmare. Usually when I lost my temper I would say anything that came into my head but this time I knew I had to retrieve the situation. I turned to Mr Biggs and looked up at him piteously. 'I didn't think working in a shoe shop would be like this,' I said, doing my damsel in distress act. 'I thought it was a − a *decent* job.'

He couldn't resist it. He straightened his drooping shoulders and stared sternly down at the boy. 'There is no reason why my assistants should be subjected to harassment,' he said. 'I must ask you to leave the shop.'

The boy grinned. 'All right, Dad,' he said cheerfully. He waved his cigarette at the bronze pedestal ashtray which stood just out of his reach and said, 'Ashtray.' I would have told him to get it himself, but poor Mr Biggs was trained to comply with the customer's wishes. He moved the ashtray within reach. The boy nipped off the glowing end of his cigarette and said, 'Who's going to put my shoe on for me?' But that was going too far. 'Nobody,' he said. 'Thought not.' He was completely unconcerned. He pushed his foot into its plimsoll and tied the lace quickly. Then he picked up his crash-helmet and got to his feet. 'Bye, Dad,' he said to Mr Biggs. 'You can go home proud today. You did your bit for the Empire.' He winked at me. 'Bye, darling. See you around.'

And suddenly I almost giggled. He wandered out, stopping to gaze at some gold evening sandals by the door as if he found them really interesting.

I fell to my knees and started gathering up shoes, gazing up at Mr Biggs appealingly. 'I won't lose my job, will I?' I asked him. 'I'm sorry I was rude but − you should have heard what he said.' I looked away modestly, managing a blush.

Mr Biggs was such a nice man, really. He said, 'Of course you won't lose your job, my dear. We musn't kow-tow to these yobboes.' He was having a good day. He even looked Mrs Marshall straight in the eye, causing her to turn away huffily. Then he marched across the carpeted floor to a massively fat, perspiring woman whose feet sprouted bunions the size of golf balls, splitting the uppers of her ancient slippers from their soles. 'Yes, madam,' he said confidently, waving her to a chair. 'Do sit down. I'm sure we can help you.' I wished him luck.

ALISON PRINCE
Goodbye Summer

From the moment he starts talking to Sasha, it is obvious the boy is determined to be difficult. Look carefully at everything he says and does in the shop and then describe the methods he uses to make himself annoying.

The novel goes on to show that after this incident Sasha cannot stop thinking about the boy. Surprisingly perhaps, she admits to herself that she found him very attractive. From what we see of him in the passage, what is there about the boy that might have appealed to Sasha?

Mrs Marshall and Sasha do not get on. What parts of the passage make this clear? Are we given any clues about why they dislike each other?

Towards the end of the passage, we are told that Mr Biggs 'was having a good day', which might seem odd in view of the scene that has just taken place in his shop. Look at the details of his involvement in the scene and try to explain why he has not been upset by it.

Answer one of the following:

How well do you think Sasha deals with the difficult situation the boy provokes? Briefly describe how her reactions to the boy and later to Mr Biggs change as the incident develops, and explain at each stage whether you feel she is approaching the situation in the right way.

We learn quite a lot from the passage about Mrs Marshall and her attitudes. Try to see what happened in the shop from her point of view and write her account of the incident as it might appear in her diary.

Sasha is working in the shoe shop as a holiday job. Imagine that next term the Careers Teacher asks her to give a short talk to her class about her experience as a shop-assistant to help them decide whether this sort of work would suit them.
Write the talk she might have given, making it clear to your audience what they might enjoy about the job as well as the difficulties they might face. The passage will suggest several ideas which could be included but you can also draw on other ideas of your own.

Your writing

Answer one of the following:

1   The last words the boy says to Sasha are 'See you around'. Invent a second meeting between the two. You can set the meeting where you wish — in the park, at a party or in a cafe, for example. Make use of what you have learnt from the passage about the two young people and try to develop the relationship.

2   First impressions are not always accurate and we can grow fond of people we did not care for at first meeting. Use this idea as the theme for a piece of writing.

   You could write, for example, a true or imaginary story in which you begin to sympathise with a 'difficult' person as you understand him or her more, or about individuals you have known and liked although they were generally considered 'awkward customers', or about yourself and the sides to you that might put people off until they come to know you better.

3   Write about a time when, like Sasha, you struggled unsuccessfully to keep your temper.

   Aim to make the reader understand the pressure you were under and the strong feelings it produced in you. What effect did your outburst have on other people and how did you feel afterwards?

You and Yours is a Radio Four programme concerned mainly with consumer matters. This item deals with misleading holiday brochures.

7
GETTING
AWAY
FROM IT ALL

Programme Presenter	Have you heard about the sleepwalker who woke up on a building site and thought he was on his holidays in Spain? The advertising blurb may be very tempting but that isn't how things always turn out. And it's not easy getting compensation. Margaret Collins has been taking up some of your cases. She heard first from Lesley Alexander, who went to Malta last summer.
Lesley Alexander	We had been led to expect that it was four-star rating and we'd assumed therefore that we'd have clean, comfortable, modern rooms with some degree of comfort. And they didn't come up to that. The food was dreadful. I think they'd tended to keep to rather cheaper cuts of meat and so on. And it was appallingly badly cooked. Having seen the children to bed, I went into our bathroom and was confronted by a cockroach. The following night the boys heard a scurrying in their room and there was a cockroach in their room too.

Margaret Collins	You might yearn for a holiday with a difference but not one quite like that. As Diana Bird explains, the Advertising Standards Authority deals with more complaints about holidays than practically any other subject.
Diana Bird	Complaints firstly about, for example, availability of flights: people ring up for flights that perhaps are advertised at £299 and find that flights are only available in January in the middle of the night and you have to go via some other destination.

Special offers which, for example, might exclude children. We get complaints that facilities are not what people expect to find — that the swimming pool or the bar or the discotheque is not functioning. Or indeed that they turn up only to find that it's a different hotel, not a quiet hotel by a nice little beach but in fact by a main road.

Frances Green   The picture looked most attractive. The pool area looked very nice. There was nothing to indicate that we were on this equivalent to an M1 motorway. It looked very, very attractive.

Margaret   Frances Green from Essex is not the first holiday-maker to have been fooled by the brochure's photograph of her luxury hotel.

Frances   It had been taken sideways on, therefore the main thoroughfare was not visible.

Margaret   What sort of a holiday did you have?

Frances   The first part of the holiday was very, very unpleasant and very, very miserable. We discovered that the bedroom, which the brochure purported to be air-conditioned, wasn't. It was very hot and very stuffy. We had a struggle to get our hotel changed and we had to incur additional cost which we hadn't budgeted for and we were really in their hands.

Margaret   Diana Bird again:

Diana   Don't believe everything you see in a brochure. There's colourful writing and colourful illustration; be sure to check the facts before you book the holiday.

Margaret   It all comes down to 'Buyer Beware' — although you're protected under the Trades Descriptions Act and the code of conduct operated by the Association of British Travel Agents. But as Nigel Coombes of the 'Travel Trade Gazette' explains, when your holiday goes wrong you're likely to feel quite alone.

Nigel Coombes   The very simple message is that you're on your own and that you have to take legal action against the travel operator when you get back to the U.K. You must take notes; you must get photographic evidence; you must talk to other people who were there on the holiday — in other words, you must get a lot of documents together and prepare yourself for a legal case. It's no good coming back and saying, 'Well, there was a motorway next door and it didn't say so in the brochure' or 'It said the swimming-pool was going to be heated and it wasn't' unless you have proof of that and you can produce that evidence when you get back.

Margaret   Which is exactly what Frances Green did when her trip to Spain found her family staying in a hotel where the grounds resembled a council rubbish tip. The remainder of her holiday was spent, not soaking up the sun, but gathering evidence.

Frances	I embarked on correspondence when I got home. Brought back a petition from people that were unfortunate enough to be in the hotel for additional weeks. They offered us £20 and I believe then they offered us £40 and I said I wanted all my money back as though that holiday hadn't taken place. Well, they wouldn't play ball on that. We sent them, I think, between ten and twelve photographs and they returned the photographs to us and were not interested.
Margaret	With no support from the holiday company, Frances turned to the Small Claims Court, who *were* interested in the photographs, accepted the evidence and awarded her a full refund and costs.

Apart from seeking redress in the Small Claims Court, the travel industry itself under the Association of British Travel Agents provides what it calls an independent conciliation service. Alan Bowen of ABTA: |
| Alan Bowen | Occasionally we find people who are looking for substantial sums of compensation where an operator has said that from his point of view there was no reason for it. If we can't conciliate there's little point in spending a long time trying to find a solution which isn't there. If, however, we have passengers who are looking for £250 and an operator has offered £125, we try and sit down and work out a sensible solution.

Now, we receive about 13,000 requests each year and on average 90 to 95 per cent of them end up in a satisfactory solution for the customer.

Occasionally we fail: either the operator's obstinate or the client's looking for something that's really unreasonable. Now, in those cases we can offer arbitration. That's administered by the Chartered Institute of Arbitrators entirely independent of ABTA. Last year 538 cases were brought, of which 411 were found in favour of the consumer. The average compensation awarded was about £275; the highest was over £3,000. |
Margaret	The cost of that service is about £25. But Nigel Coombes of 'The Travel Trade Gazette' says that the Small Claims Court might be a better way.
Nigel	The better way in my view — because I don't think ABTA is always as independent as it likes to think — is to take action in the Small Claims Court. But the same advice stands: Do get your evidence while you're there. It's no good coming back and saying, 'Well, this happened' because the court official will just say, 'Well, can you prove that please?'
Programme Presenter	All that information about holidays is in this week's fact sheet. You can get your copy by writing to 'You and Yours', Broadcasting House, London W1A 1AA.

Guaranteed SUN and Guaranteed FUN

ACAPULCO APTS

As the dawn breaks and the sun peaks over the horizon to the east. the main benefit of staying in the Acapulco becomes obvious - it 's only a five minute walk from the Veronicas nightlife of Las Americas.

In fact the Acapulco is a good all round Club base. The apartments here are comfortable. with private facilities. balconies and fully equipped kitchenettes. There is an excellent pool with a large sunbathing terrace equipped with sunbeds. or the beach is nearby.

There is a bar and restaurant here serving snacks and drinks at very reasonable prices and a full restaurant menu at night. There is also a video player. 2 pool tables and a good sound system.

All in all the Acapulco is perfectly placed for you to enjoy the best of Las Americas. The sun. the sea. the beach. the nightlife and a range of bars and restaurants are on the doorstep.

Supplements per person per week: In an apartment for 3. 2 sharing £8.00 (£14.00). Supplements in brackets apply to July and August departures. **No supplements for departures up to 31 May or after 1 October.**
Meals: Self catering.

Not that long ago there was nothing at all on this particular part of Tenerife's south coast. Then somebody noticed the fact that the weather here is fantastic all the year round, spotted the great beaches and decided to build a hotel or two. From that day on, Playa de las Americas has never looked back.

It's the ultimate in designer resorts, one enormous pleasure garden dedicated to give as much as possible to as many as possible in as small an area as possible.

For young people, the main attractions are not those of the daylight hours, because this is the 'latest' resort we've ever seen. Generally the action doesn't get going until past midnight but then the resort rocks right through until the discos close at around 6am! What's more, so that you don't have to walk too far to get from place to place, the whole nightlife is crammed into one strip no more than 400 metres long, which has bars, cafés and discos on 4 levels, and is the most futuristic place on earth, just like one enormous night club with over 200 bars and fifty dance floors.

You can start with a cocktail at Waikiki, slip downstairs to Sgt Peppers for a dance, bop again in Bonker's Fun Club which has one of the craziest DJ's in Las Americas, and you've still not even scratched the surface of the place. Nobody goes to bed much before 5am, and time means absolutely nothing.

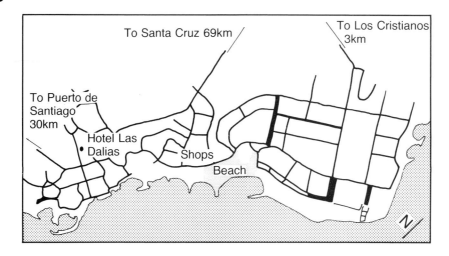

The rapidly-developing and ever popular Playa de las Americas lies on the south coast of Tenerife and is a purpose-built resort with a relaxed and easy-going atmosphere. It has a dark sand beach, attractive gardens and delightful promenades as well as plenty of shops, bars, cafés and restaurants in which you may enjoy "international" as well as more traditional local dishes.

Approximate transfer time from Reina Sofia Airport: 30 mins.

Hotel Las Dalias

◆◆◆◆

IN OUR OPINION "Las Dalias, situated in a quieter part of the resort, offers a very good standard of service, accommodation and a varied entertainments programme."

LOCATION It is set in the new residential area of Playa de las Americas and it is a downhill walk from the resort's busy centre and seafront promenade.

AMENITIES Throughout the hotel the accent is on elegance and spaciousness. The lounges and bars are tastefully decorated and have an informal atmosphere, with an entertainments programme which will appeal to those looking for quality enjoyment. For your relaxation and refreshment there are two swimming pools, one crossed by a narrow bridge, and both are surrounded by extensive terraces.

MEALS The informal modern restaurant offers a cooked breakfast, and a beautifully presented buffet for lunch. Buffet and waiter service at dinner. **Half Board.**

BEDROOMS with two or three beds, private bathroom with bath, shower and balcony.

Official rating: 4 stars, 430 rooms, 3 lifts.

Supplements for single room and **reductions for 3rd adult** are in the Price List.

GOLDEN DAYS CLUB
Yours To Enjoy

A warm welcome from your resident Golden Days host or host couple who will organise a superb variety of activities and entertainment.
- Welcome party with free drink
- Guided walk around your resort
- Free membership of our Newspaper and Magazine Club
- Walks and rambles to local places of interest
- Library of English books
- Cards and board games
- Quizzes and competitions
- Lady Intasun Competition – win a bottle of 'bubbly'
- Sequence, old tyme, ballroom and modern dancing
- Evening entertainments most evenings
- Christmas and New Year Gala dinners
- Pool table, table tennis and darts
- Keep fit, squash
- Party Night with competitions and games
- Occasional English video

Special Offers
- Free bottle of wine per room
- Free tea and biscuits daily

Tenerife

Altamar
Apartments

SSS

FREE
GROCERY
·PACK·

These white, two-storey buildings are surrounded by well cared-for shrubs and flower beds that provide a blaze of colour. This really is the place to choose if you want to spend your self-catering holiday in an attractive setting. And though they are on a quiet road towards the back of the resort, the apartments are only about 500 yards from the lively Veronica Centre and it's just another 100 yards to the beach.

◆ Swimming pool with sun terrace

◆ Bar and restaurant five minutes' walk away

◆ Supermarket next door

◆ Snack bar within complex

◆ Small children's pool

◆ Cot hire and highchairs available

◆ Maid service six times a week

◆ FREE grocery pack included

This is sun-soaked southern Tenerife's favourite resort. It's a stylish blend of palm-lined seafront promenades and wide avenues, with exciting shopping and relaxed open-air cafés. Kiddies love the sandy beaches and the recently opened WaterPark, and there's plenty of windsurfing, sailing and tennis. After dark you'll find lots of discos and nightclubs to keep you happy well into the early hours.

Understanding

1 Describe briefly the differences between what the two holiday-makers in the *You and Yours* item expected and what they found on their holidays.

2 How can you tell that most of what the reporter, Margaret Collins, says in the programme is being read from a script she has prepared beforehand, whereas the holiday-makers, Lesley Alexander and Frances Green, are working out what they say as they go along?

3 In the radio programme, Diana Bird says: 'Don't believe everything you see in a brochure. There is colourful writing and colourful illustration.' Explain what you think she means by 'colourful writing and colourful illustration', using examples from the brochures on pages 43 to 45 to help you make your points.

4 The three brochure extracts advertise holidays at the same resort, Playa de las Americas, but each brochure is targeted at a different sort of client. Basing your answer on the way the brochures are written and the information they contain, describe the typical holiday-maker each one is trying to attract.

Response

Answer one of the following:

1 Here is one person's reaction to the *You and Yours* item:

The BBC dredge up a couple of moaning wet blankets who were looking for a five-star holiday on the cheap, get them to whine about a few petty grievances, add one or two 'experts' to back them up and so produce yet another biased attack on the British travel industry.

Referring closely to the programme, say whether you agree with this opinion of it.

2 At the end of the radio programme the presenter invites listeners to write in for a fact sheet. This will sum up clearly the advice given in the programme and outline the action people can take if they have a complaint about their holiday.
   Produce your own version of the fact sheet, extracting from the programme whatever information and advice you think are important.

3 You take one of the holidays advertised on pages 43 to 45 and it is a great disappointment – nothing like the brochure promised. Write a letter of complaint to the travel operator, referring to what the brochure led you to expect and what you discovered when you got there.

Plan the tone of your letter carefully. You will want to make clear how annoyed you are and insist on some form of compensation, but should you go further and get really angry or use cutting sarcasm? You must decide the approach that is most likely to achieve fast results. On page 123 you will find advice on how to set out this sort of formal letter.

Your writing

Answer one of the following:

1 Write about holidays and outings you have actually taken, imagining you are recording your thoughts as you look through a photograph album. You pause over particular pictures as they call to mind places, people and incidents from the past. Some of them make pleasant memories, others you would rather forget.

2 Sometimes it is the unexpected that makes a holiday successful. You meet someone by chance or you discover a place not mentioned in the brochures and suddenly what looked like being a very ordinary few days becomes a time you will always treasure.

   Write a short story about a holiday of this kind, perhaps based on your own experience.

3 Produce two well-designed extracts from different holiday brochures, one meant for people your age and a little older, the other for middle-aged or elderly holiday-makers. In both extracts, you should try to 'market' your own area as a tremendous place for a holiday — which might be a real challenge!

   The brochures on pages 43 to 45 will give you a good idea of the style of writing to aim at, but remember you are trying to attract two very different types of customer.

8
DON'T
GO NEAR
THE
WATER

The Lake

For years there have been no fish in the lake.
People hurrying through the park avoid it
like the plague. Birds steer clear
and the sedge of course has withered.
Trees lean away from it,
and at night it reflects, not the moon,
but the blackness of its own depths.
There are no fish in the lake.
But there is life there. There is life . . .

Underwater pigs glide between reefs of coral debris.
They love it here. They breed and multiply
in sties hollowed out of the mud
and lined with mattresses and bedsprings.
They live on dead fish and rotting things,
drowned pets, plastic and assorted excreta.
Rusty cans they like the best.
Holding them in webbed trotters
their teeth tear easily through the tin,
and poking in a snout, they noisily suck out
the putrid matter within.

There are no fish in the lake.
But there is life there. There is life . . .

For on certain evenings after dark
shoals of pigs surface
and look out at those houses near the park.
Where, in bathrooms,
children feed stale bread to plastic ducks,
and in attics,
toy yachts have long since runaground.
Where, in livingrooms,
anglers dangle their lines on patterned carpets,
and bemoan the fate of the ones that got away.

Down on the lake, piggy eyes glisten.
They have acquired a taste for flesh.
They are licking their lips. Listen . . .

ROGER McGOUGH

DOES THE CAMERA LIE? This photograph was taken in 1977 by Antony Shiels, from Urquhart Castle, Scotland.

THE LOCH'S ELUSIVE MONSTER

An underwater camera may have solved the 1400 yea enigma

Loch Ness, in Scotland, is the reputed home of a monster that has been chronicled, with varying degrees of credibility, over the past 1400 years. The loch is the largest sheet of fresh water in Britain and perhaps the most sinister, even when the sun shines on its murky, peat-stained waters.

Those waters are so deep – more than 900 feet in parts – that they would engulf most of the world's tallest buildings.

Some of the stories about th Loch Ness Monster appear equall tall. The earliest of them goes bac to about AD 565, when the monste was said to have been sighted by th Irish saint, Columba. According t his biographer, St Adamnan, writ ing a century later, a disciple c Columba was swimming across th mile-wide loch, to fetch a boat fo his master from the opposite shor when the monster suddenly rose t the surface 'with a great roar an open mouth'.

The onlookers, converts and heathen alike, were, according to Adamnan, 'stricken with very great terror'. But St Columba, making the sign of the Cross and invoking the Almighty, is said to have repelled the monster with the words: 'Think not to go further, nor touch thou that man. Quick, go back . . .' The beast obeyed, and has never hurt anyone since.

Adamnan's account may have been a powerful argument for the power of prayer, but it was somewhat vague as a portrait of the monster. Indeed, no clear picture of it emerged until 14 centuries – and innumerable sightings – later. Then, in 1933, a London surgeon, driving past the loch on holiday, secured the first photograph of a monster – or what was claimed to be one. It showed a long neck, arched over the water from a thick body and was taken, according to the surgeon, from a distance of 200 to 300 yards, near Invermoriston.

At that point, the road runs 200 feet above the loch. The road was then newly built, which may have had some kind of connection with the spate of sightings reported around that time. There were frequent explosions as engineers blasted a path for the road.

Did the noise disturb the monster from the depths of the loch? Or was it just that, with the coming of the road, new vistas were opened up, enabling tourists to see, for the first time in centuries, something that had always been living in the water? Whatever the answer, the first photograph was published in the London *Daily Mail* and provoked an argument that was to rage for years.

Sceptics claim that it portrays either a mass of decaying vegetable matter, lifted to the surface by trapped gases, or the tip of the tail

The first photograph taken in 1933.

of a diving otter photographed out of scale.

On the other hand, true believers in the monster say that the picture tallies with the description given by many people who claim to have seen the creature and that, in any case, an eminent surgeon would hardly be likely to risk his reputation for a hoax.

The last argument may indicate a touching faith in the medical profession. All the same, it remains a fact that many of the people who are convinced they have seen the monster belong to groups normally considered to be truthful witnesses: schoolmasters, naval officers, Benedictine monks, a Nobel prizewinner, two town clerks and many dour Scottish professional men, none of them inclined by nature to risk ridicule or to court publicity for its own sake.

While naturalists and zoologists tended to steer clear of the argument, bolder spirits pressed on with the search for more evidence. Sometimes this appeared to those who were not looking, such as Lachlan Stuart, a forestry worker who lived beside the loch. In 1951 when he went out one morning at 6.30 to milk his cows he noticed a disturbance on the water, and three humps appeared, moving in line towards the shore.

Stuart ran back to the house and grabbed his small box camera and a family friend to back up the evidence of his own eyes. He managed to take one picture before the monster (if such it was) vanished and the camera shutter jammed.

Stuart's picture, taken from a range of 60 yards, got wide publicity, as the surgeon's had done 18 years before. But by and large, people remained sceptical of this and other photographical evidence.

The first moving pictures of something that might have been 'Nessie', as the monster was now affectionately known, came in 1960. The cameraman was Tim Dinsdale, an aviation engineer, who was so convinced of his film's authenticity that he gave up his career to live in a small boat on the loch, in full-time pursuit of the elusive monster.

Dinsdale's enthusiasm fired others, and helped to pave the way for a more scientific approach to the question of whether or not the monster really exists. In 1961, the Loch Ness Phenomena Investigation Bureau was formed, at the instigation of two naturalists and David James, a Member of Parliament, who became the bureau's organiser.

He collated, checked and published all the reports of sightings and enlisted students and other volunteers to man, during the summer months, the 36-inch cameras set up at strategic points around the 24-mile loch.

The range of one camera overlapped the next, so that observation was complete – as well as continuous. But the evidence they yielded has been inconclusive. So has that of British and Japanese television crews, who hoped to record the monster's activities with the aid of the most modern scientific equipment.

One such expedition, in 1969, deployed the Vicker's submersible Pisces, with low-light-level underwater cameras, closed-circuit TV and videotape recording machines. There was also a one-man American submarine, the Viperfish, and a team of sonar experts. Elevated cameras constantly covered the surface during the day, and a 'night-sight' camera was used for ship patrols after dark.

More bizarre items of equipment included a noise-making machine, lent by the Royal Navy, with which it was hoped to disturb the monster. In addition, an evil-smelling bait of suitably monstrous proportions was dangled in the loch. The bait weighed half a hundredweight, and was compounded of dried animal blood, snake hormone and other fearsome ingredients which it was hoped might have some appeal to 'Nessie'.

But the beast remained coy as ever. No sight or sound of her appeared on either camera or sonar gear, and this particular expedition's sole contribution to the world's knowledge of 'Nessie' and her habitat came from the submersible Pisces. Diving off Castle Urquart, her crew took a sounding which showed the loch to be 950 feet deep at that point – 200 feet deeper than was supposed. The Pisces, on this dive, also found a vast underwater cavern.

The monster's lair? Maybe – but of the monster, no sign. The expedition left, with its leader lamenting that, for him, it was the 'end of a legend'.

In November 1975, however, an American research team produced new photographic evidence that impressed sceptical experts and caused Sir Peter Scott, the

his picture was taken by Hugh Gray in 1933.

aturalist, to say that the monster xisted.

Mr Robert Rines, president of he Massachusetts Academy of Applied Sciences, led the team that perated a 16mm motor-driven amera, suspended 45 feet below a oat, and took pictures by earchlight every 75 seconds.

Several seemed to show a ed-brown beast about 12 feet ong, with a hideous head and an rching neck about 8 feet long. Mr ames proclaimed that they stablished the monster's existence eyond reasonable doubt', and ppealed unsuccessfully to the ritish Government to protect it nder the Conservation of Wild reatures Act.

Many experts, although impressed, said the evidence was far from conclusive, but Sir Peter was convinced that a family of prehistoric plesiosaurs — a species of fish-eating reptiles that had been officially extinct for 70 million years — had survived or could have survived in the loch.

The monster's advocates have always argued that when the last Ice Age ended, 10,000—15,000 years ago, sea levels must have been raised considerably by the melting ice. Floodwater could have swept a number of plesiosaurs into the newly formed loch.

Strange Stories, Amazing Facts
from *Readers Digest*

Understanding

1 What does Roger McGough make the readers of his poem fee about the lake and the pigs that live in it? How does he do this? Look carefully at the details he includes in the poem as well as the words he uses to describe them.

2 Some readers of the poem might not have realised it is mean as a serious warning against pollution. What would you point out about the poem to make them see it in this way?

3 Suppose someone expressed the following opinion about the Loch Ness Monster:

Nobody in their right mind believes what a few attention-seeking cranks tell them about a fantastic science-fiction monster which manages, in some miraculous way, to stay well hidden in such a small stretch of water.

This statement can be broken down into a number of points all of which would be denied by people who believe in the monster. What facts in the article on pages 50 – 53 could they use to answer these particular points?

4 It would be wrong for an article like this one to take sides on whether there really is a Loch Ness Monster. How well do you think the author has managed to keep his or her own personal views hidden from the reader? Give clear reasons for your answer, quoting from the article where necessary.

Response

Answer one of the following:

1 Has the article on the Loch Ness Monster made you more o less ready to believe that Nessie exists? You should refer closely to things said in the article and also say how convincing you find the photographs.

2 Your school holds a debate on the Loch Ness Monster. Ther are two main speakers. One argues that there is more than enough evidence for the existence of the monster, the othe denies this.

After the audience has had an opportunity to air its views the main speakers are given two or three minutes each to sum up their key points so that they are fresh in people's minds when the vote is taken.

Basing your work on the article, write these two short speeches. This is the last chance each speaker has to sway the audience so it is important they present their argumen in a clear, forceful way.

3 The 1969 Loch Ness expedition is described on page 52. Imagine you are a journalist whose job it is to write a shor news article about the expedition soon after the leader announces it has been wound up.

You happen to believe the expedition has been a stupid waste of time and money. You cannot actually state this opinion in your article because it is meant to be a straight factual report. However, your feelings will certainly affect the *tone* of what you write and the way you report the facts. You will find suggestions on how to write a newspaper article on page 121.

Roger McGough's poems are very popular with young people. *The Lake* is a typical example of his work. Referring closely to the poem, say why you think it would appeal to young readers.

Your writing

Answer one of the following:

The Lake ends with the pigs looking longingly towards the nearby houses. Continue the story, making use of what you have learnt about the appearance, behaviour and intentions of the creatures in the poem.

We know, if only from books and films, how strange, beautiful and dangerous the world below the surface of deep lakes and oceans can be. Take 'The Wonders and Perils of the Deep' as your theme and develop it in any way that interests you. You could, for example, write factually on the subject if you know enough about it, or tell a story of underwater exploration, or try, in a poem perhaps, to create a picture of fantastic landscape and weird creatures.

Roger McGough's poem is a striking way of underlining the dangers of pollution. What are your own views on the problem? Are we really putting our future at risk? If so, what practical steps can be taken to reduce the danger?

This is a very wide topic. A full discussion would need to consider litter and the disposal of human, industrial and nuclear waste, the damage to the ozone layer by aerosol and other gases, the health risks from car exhausts, pesticides and fertilizers, and several other matters. It may be better to limit your discussion to just one or two types of pollution.

9

ONE ARMED BANDITS

This letter appeared in the *Readers' Opinions* column of a national newspaper:

Dear Editor

As you rightly say in your article 'Gambling: the British disease' (7th May), this country has indeed been suffering an epidemic of gambling fever in recent years. What you do not make clear, however, is that this crippling disease is caught at a frighteningly early age. I refer, of course, to the fruit machine mania that has our young people so firmly in its grip.

No longer are these machines restricted to arcades and private clubs. They are everywhere now: in sports and leisure centres, fish and chip shops, cafés and take-aways — even sweet shops. Our youngsters are being cruelly subjected to an enormous temptation.

And we need only look around us to see that the majority of our children are completely unable to resist the temptation. Most of them appear to be hopelessly hooked on these evil machines and cannot let a day go by without satisfying a craving just as destructive as heroin or cocaine addiction.

The average youngster 'plays' for literally hours at a time, delivering up what seems to be an endless supply of coins to these 'one-armed bandits'. I cannot help wondering where boys and girls still at school come by the large sums of money needed to feed their habit.

This urgent social problem requires immediate action. 'The British disease' will be brought under control only when we tackle its early stages and place much tighter restrictions on where fruit machines can be located and who can use them.

Yours faithfully,
L. BARREN
(Birmingham)

A recent Government report looked into this question of young people and fruit machines. The report was based on a survey of 2,000 girls and boys aged ten to sixteen. These are some of the findings:

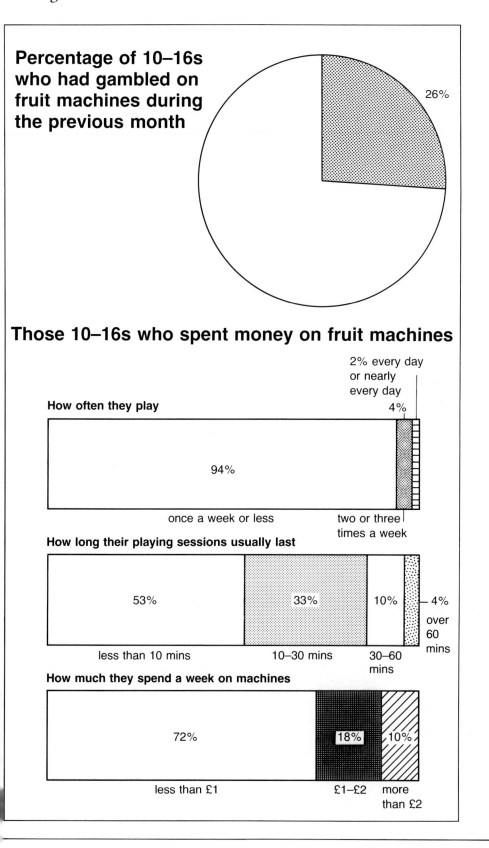

Percentage of 10–16s who had gambled on fruit machines during the previous month

26%

Those 10–16s who spent money on fruit machines

How often they play

2% every day or nearly every day

4%

94%

once a week or less

two or three times a week

How long their playing sessions usually last

53%

33%

10%

4% over 60 mins

less than 10 mins

10–30 mins

30–60 mins

How much they spend a week on machines

72%

18%

10%

less than £1

£1–£2

more than £2

These comments were made by young people who do play
arcade machines regularly:

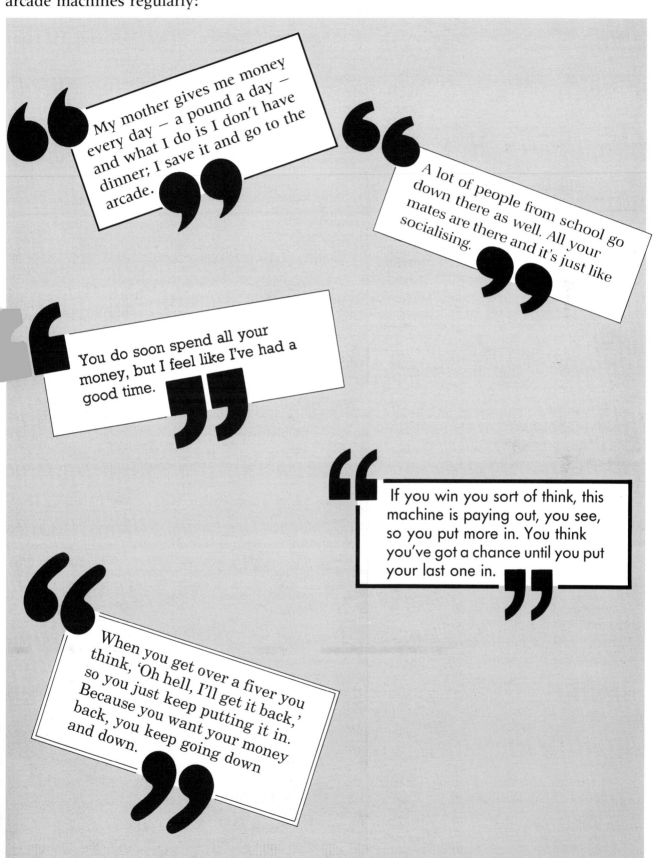

"My mother gives me money every day – a pound a day – and what I do is I don't have dinner; I save it and go to the arcade."

"A lot of people from school go down there as well. All your mates are there and it's just like socialising."

"You do soon spend all your money, but I feel like I've had a good time."

"If you win you sort of think, this machine is paying out, you see, so you put more in. You think you've got a chance until you put your last one in."

"When you get over a fiver you think, 'Oh hell, I'll get it back,' so you just keep putting it in. Because you want your money back, you keep going down and down."

"It's great when your friends are standing around, and you're getting the highest score, getting through the scenes. If you get a top score, you put your name on it so everybody sees you've won."

"I feel disgusted with myself when I lose; I feel stupid. I've spent all my money and I just think, 'Oh God! how pathetic I am.'"

"I know this lad who lost ninety quid in the arcade and I'm not kidding; probably his mum sent him out shopping for clothes – he wanted some shoes or something – and then he goes and blows it all in the arcade. That's why he nicked the clothes from the shop."

"If you do start going down to the arcade, even if you're with an OK group who don't smoke, you're bound to get to know people who do smoke and I suppose in a way they will start you off."

1   According to Mr Barren's letter on page 56, why are there more young gamblers than there used to be?

2   Obviously Mr Barren wants his readers to feel just as worried about fruit machines as he does, and the way he writes about the situation does make it seem very serious indeed.

    Look at how he expresses himself – the words and phrases he uses to describe the problem. How does he try to get us to see it as an urgent and frightening matter?

3   In paragraphs three and four of his letter, Mr Barren makes a number of statements about how heavily involved young people are with fruit machines. Check what he says against the government statistics on page 57 and then explain clearly where he is mistaken.

4   Study the comments on pages 59 and 60. What do we learn from them about why some young people spend so much time and money in arcades?

5   Judging by their comments, what are the possible harmful effects these young people are facing?

Answer one of the following:

1   Although you may agree with Mr Barren that some restrictions need to be placed on fruit machines, you will have seen how he exaggerates the size of the problem. Write a letter for publication in the same newspaper, in which you attempt to correct the very black picture he paints.

    In your reply you should refer to the statistics on page 57, but a mass of figures may just confuse the reader. Give only those that are important for your case. One thing that can be said for Mr Barren's letter is that it is clear and lively. You should aim to make yours the same.

    Treat this as a formal letter and read the suggestions on page 123 before you begin.

2   Imagine a radio 'phone-in' on the subject of gambling. Mr Barren rings to voice his concern about young people and fruit machines. The 'expert' in the studio knows the statistics on the subject and is not convinced the problem is as serious as Mr Barren claims. How might the conversation go?

    Set your work out as a script. Page 124 will help you to do this. The dialogue should sound natural, so avoid long set speeches.

Your writing

Answer one of the following:

1   Making use of ideas suggested to you by the comments on pages 59 and 60 and any relevant personal experience you have, write a piece of description, possibly a poem, set in an amusement arcade.

  You can concentrate your description on one particular individual or give an interesting general impression of the whole scene.

2   We know that any form of addiction or obsession can ruin lives. Gambling, drinking, drug-taking and solvent-abuse are obvious examples, but there are other ways people can become their own victims. The obsession with staying slim that is called *anorexia nervosa*, uncontrollable aggression or even extreme shyness can all spoil a person's life.

  Tell the story of someone who has this sort of problem. You may stay with the topic of teenage gambling and write about one of the teenagers quoted on pages 59 and 60, or if you prefer, choose one of the other kinds of victim just mentioned.

  A subject like this needs very sensitive handling. Your treatment should help readers to understand the person's feelings and how desperately sad such a case can be.

3   You may think Mr Barren's letter is typical of the way older people see only the worst in your generation. If so, write about the 'generation gap' from this point of view, discussing the different types of accusation made against people your age and explaining why you think they are unfair.

THE LITTLE PALACE

We both knew at once when the removal van arrived, at ten o'clock, on the Saturday morning because there were no curtains at the windows and it was so big that it shut out almost all the light as it stopped on the damp cobbles outside the house. I said, 'Here they are, Tom,' and got up from my knees beside the tea-chest into which I'd been carefully packing the most fragile of our crockery.

Tom looked down from where, standing on a chair, he was dismantling the cupboards over the sink: the cupboards he had intended leaving behind had the new tenants not turned out to be the sort of people they were. The first thing anyone noticed about Tom, I suppose, was his size. He wore his fair hair cut short and he had blue eyes in a guileless, pug-nosed face. The numerous mishaps, small, thank God, sustained in his work as a coal miner were recorded in the faint blue scars on the backs of his hands: hands that were big and calloused and rough to the touch: hands that could be so unbelievably gentle and tender when touching me.

'I reckon everything else is ready, Janie,' he said now. 'I'll be done here in a jiffy.'

I often wondered when people glanced at us when we were together what they made of Tom and me. Tom so big and so obviously a man of toil and sweat, and me so *petite*, with looks that Tom thought so pretty and lady-like and I'd always considered insipid; Tom with his voice heavy with the West Riding, and mine from which my mother and the elocution teacher she had sent me to had coaxed all trace of locality in my childhood. I'd heard one of Tom's sisters refer to me as 'The Duchess' when I wasn't supposed to hear, but I'd learned to hold my own with them, and Tom, when I'd told him about it, said it was a compliment, and if I wasn't proud of it, he was.

I opened the door as one of the men knocked.

'Manage it in one trip easy,' Tom said as the two men stepped over the threshold and looked around with experienced eyes. There wasn't a lot. We had been married only a year, and the house was very small: one room up, one down.

As the men started to carry out the furniture I slipped on a coat and went outside; partly to be out of their way, and partly to watch that they did not mishandle anything as they packed it into the gaping interior of the van. And as I stood there on the pavement I felt a hidden audience watching from the cover of lace curtains. I knew I had disappointed and antagonised some of our neighbours by not encouraging them to run in and out of my house as they did one another's; and now the more inquisitive would be snatching a last look at what they had merely glimpsed as it came into the house a year ago. Mrs Wilde from the next house below came out on to the step. Her face was unwashed, her hair uncombed. She stood with her arms folded across her grubby pinafore, her bare toes poking out of worn felt slippers. When I thought about it I could not remember ever having seen her in a pair of shoes.

'Well, off you go to leave us, Mrs Green,' she said amiably.

'Yes,' I said, 'off we go, Mrs Wilde.' She had been into the house several times, and there was little strange for her to see.

'Don't seem hardly two minutes sin' ye got here,' she said, relaxing into her favourite stance against the door jamb.

'No, time flies.'

'It does that,' she said. 'It does that! Bought your own place over t'new part o' town, so I hear?'

'Yes, that's right, Mrs Wilde. A semi-detached on Laburnum Rise.'

She nodded. 'Aye, aye. I reckon that'll be more your quarter like than over here. I mean, this is nowt new to yer husband. I've known his fam'ly for years, an' they've allus been collier-fowk. But I knew straightaway 'at you were used to summat better. You can tell fowk at's had good bringin's up. Leastways, I allus can.'

I made no reply to this. I didn't know what to say. For what Mrs Wilde said was true: I hadn't been used to this kind of neighbourhood until my marriage; but I'd become accustomed by now to at least one small part of it — the house Tom and I called home. The first home we ever had.

'You certainly made t'best on it, though,' Mrs Wilde was saying. 'I wouldn't ha' recognised t'place if I hadn't lived right next door. A proper little palace you made on it — a proper little palace. That's just what I said to my husband when I first saw inside. Such a shame an' all 'at you've to leave it in one way: after all t'work you put into it. All the lovely decorations. Must break your heart to leave 'em all to some'dy else.' She paused and cocked an inquisitive eye at me.

'Course, anybody fair like 'ud be only too willing to make it right with you . . . I mean, it's only proper an' decent, in't it?*

I did not respond to her probing, but merely remarked, 'Yes, you can usually come to some agreement.' I did not feel inclined to summon up her sympathy by telling her that the new tenants, a cold-faced elderly couple, had refused even to consider the question of compensation. And of course there was nothing to be done about it: we had no legal claim for improvements done to someone else's property. It had made Tom very angry and he had almost quarrelled with the elderly man.

'Perhaps they aren't very well off,' I'd said afterwards. 'Or why should they want a poky little place like this at their age?'

'Oh, you're too soft by half, Janie,' Tom had said. 'You'd let anybody put on you . . . No, its meanness, that's what it is. I could see it in the way their faces sort o' closed up the minute I mentioned valuation. You can bet your life they're not short o' brass. They're not sort to spend any 'less they're forced to.' He had stopped speaking then to consider the situation. 'Well, we can take the cupboards an' shelves I put up, I suppose. A bit o' timber allus comes in handy. But we can't take the wallpaper an' paint. They'll have the benefit of that, damn their stingy souls!'

'Yes, it's only right an' proper,' Mrs Wilde said.

We had arranged that I should go with the van and direct the unloading of the furniture, then come back for Tom, who had one or two last jobs to do, when we would go on for lunch with his family. When the loading was finished, then, I gave the driver the address of our new house and climbed up into the cab, where they made room for me between them. It was only a ten-minute drive across town, but it was to me like a journey into another world: my own world of neat houses along tree-lined backwaters and the Sunday-afternoon quiet of sheltered gardens. It was the sort of district that

* When people move into rented accommodation they will often decide, out of a sense of fairness, to pay something to the previous tenants for any improvements they have made.

people in books and plays scoffed at as dull and suburban. But people like that, I thought, had never lived in a place like Bridge Street. But though it was my own world, and the thought of living there again was very pleasant, there was yet no place in it I could call home: not as I regarded the Little Palace (as we called the house, after Mrs Wilde) as home. I thought as the men began to unload at the end of the short drive, of how that once strange and dirty place had become almost like a part of me, so that ever since waking that morning, and before, there had been in me a vague melancholy at the prospect of leaving it. I had chided myself for my foolish fancies, but it was almost as though I felt that the house was a part of our luck, and that in leaving it we might also leave something of our happiness within its walls.

For we had been happy there, gloriously happy. And not much more than a year ago

I had not even seen the house. A little over two years ago there had been nothing — not even Tom. And what was there in life now without him? Tom, who had appeared and shattered the cocoon which my parents' genteel, middle-class way of life had spun about me and taught me to live as I never had before. It seemed strange to me that I had hardly been alive at all until that strange, disturbing afternoon when I first noticed him from the office window as, tired and dirty, he crossed the yard from the pit-hill at the end of the shift . . .

I tipped the two men when they had finished, and then walked through the house from room to room, seeing how lost our furniture looked in it, and noting with my woman's eye all the things that needed to be done. And then I left the house and walked to the bus stop at the end of the avenue. There was a sneaking chill in the air and I felt in its touch the end of the glorious but all-too-short summer.

The sun was shining, the sky blue, the day I had met Tom. Two days after my first noticing him he came into the big new building, with its many area control offices, to see the manager and blundered into the wrong office, and so into my life. It was like nothing I had ever known before, that feeling which possessed me from then on; it flushed my cheeks at the thought of him, brought tremors to my hands and knees, and filled me with a breathless, delighted excitement. And from that first brief contact, when I came into the corridor to show him the door he wanted, grew Tom's awareness of me. His eyes began to seek me out as he crossed the yard at the end of the day shift, and soon we were openly exchanging smiles. Even though we did not speak to each other again for some time a kind of intimacy seemed to grow between us through the medium of those daily smiles; so that one day when I had occasion to leave the office early, not long after the change of shifts, it seemed very natural when he came roaring up the yard behind me on his motor cycle that he should offer me a lift into town, and that I should at once accept. That was the day he asked me, with almost painful shyness, to go out with him one evening, and the day I became hopelessly lost. Three months later, to his open astonishment, I accepted his halting proposal of marriage.

And all this was what the Little Palace had come to mean to me. More, much more, than the cleanliness and shining paint had emerged from the squalor of flaking plaster and peeling wallpaper that had been the house when first we took it. A marriage had been made there, had come through its first vital year; a marriage that had received little but discouragement because of the differences between Tom and me. I was too good for him, they had said. I was throwing myself away on a boy from the back streets whose rough-shod nature and way of living would sooner or later break my heart. But they had been wrong; only the walls of the Little Palace knew how wrong. Those walls had held our year of hope and happiness;

our failures, and, above all, our success. It was because of this that I knew I should remember it for the rest of my life.

I alighted from the bus and, absorbed in these thoughts, I had walked right into the living-room before I saw what awaited me there. And then I stood and gaped in staggered disbelief. The room was as though emblazoned with warnings of a terrible plague; for on each of the walls, stretching diagonally from ceiling to floor across the pale blue wallpaper, and on each of the doors, Tom had painted a huge scarlet cross. And now, brush in hand, he spoke to me over his shoulder as he heard me come in.

'Janie? Little surprise for you. An' a damn big 'un for them two stingy old codgers when they turn up again.'

I turned without answering and ran out of the room and up the uncarpeted stairs into the bedroom. He had done that room first. I came slowly down again. My heart hurt as though a great hand was kneading it brutally and I couldn't speak.

'Thought of it yesterday,' Tom said. He was putting on his jacket now and he wore a grin which slowly faded as he saw the expression on my face. 'Well, I mean, damn it, we couldn't let 'em get away with it altogether, could we?'

I shook my head. 'No, Tom.'

'Damn it,' Tom said again, 'it serves 'em right for bein' so flamin' mean!'

He wrapped the paint-brush in a piece of rag and put it in his pocket. 'They can have the paint.' He looked at me. 'C'mon, then, let's be off. Take your last look at this place. You won't be seein' it any more.'

We went out, he closing and locking the door behind us, and walked away together. It was about half-way down the street, that, to Tom's confusion and distress, I began to cry.

'What's up, Janie?' He stopped and peered down at me. 'What's wrong, love?'

But I could only shake my head in reply. It was going to be all right. I just knew it was. But I couldn't help but cry.

STAN BARSTOW

MOVING HOUSE

Like a life that dies on a summer's afternoon,
The blood in the veins of the house
Is weakening now. Was strong and thick
In the arteries, and thicker still
In the children's songs.
The inquisitive sun is sprinkling light
On the chairs, the tables, the cups and plates,
And the strange black van that is waiting.

There were doors in the house that opened
Only at times, for the keys were lost.
But the other doors swung on their hinges
And the rooms became worn to the shape
Of the lives that fitted them.

There were faces that drifted out of the mists
Surrounding us, stayed for a time, became
Part of the mood that was governing us.
Now are blurred into the cherry tree's flowering,
Or preserved in a dream that recurs.

Now the rooms are all disordered by emptiness,
Sudden exposure of dust and paint that is peeling.
In the drive an armchair sags in the sunlight,
And holly and yew are sheltering things
Like displaced persons, all huddled and bruised
Waiting their next rough handling.

                              HEATHER BUCK

Understanding

1 In *The Little Palace*, we are told that Janie's and Tom's families did not approve of their marriage. According to the story, why did each side object?

2 Janie says that Laburnum Rise 'was only a ten-minute drive across town, but it was to me like a journey into another world.' What are the differences between Bridge Street and the new neighbourhood which make her see them as worlds apart?

3 Why do you suppose Janie is so upset by what her husband has done to the house and why, in the last sentence, does she seem to need to reassure herself that everything is going to be all right?

4 In the poem, *Moving House*, Heather Buck is also moving away from somewhere that has been her home for a long time. What emotions and thoughts does she have about the place she is leaving?

5 Do you see any similarities between Heather Buck's feeling for her house and those Janie has for the 'Little Palace'?

Response

Answer one of the following:

1 In several ways Tom is a very different person from Janie. If he read *The Little Palace*, he would probably agree with many of his wife's views, but some of her ideas and feelings he might find hard to understand.

   Imagine you are Tom and write your reactions to the story, making use of what you have learnt about his character and attitudes. Refer closely to things your wife says and make clear, for example, whether you feel the same about the 'Little Palace' and Laburnum Rise as Janie does. Now you have read the story, can you see why what you did made her cry?

2 After the elderly couple move in and discover the state of their new home, they write to Tom. Something they say in their letter shows him he has completely misjudged them. He now finds it embarrassing to write a reply, but forces himself to do so.

   Write your own version of these two letters, deciding for yourself what it is that changes Tom's mind about the couple.

3 Suppose that Heather Buck records in her diary that evening her thoughts about leaving the old house. The poem indicates in a general way how she felt, but in the diary she is much more precise and detailed.

Write the entry she might have made, including in it the sort of memories you think would be uppermost in her mind that day.

Answer one of the following:

1   In Stan Barstow's story we see that even when two people are in love, differences of background and attitude can create problems. We are left wondering whether, in the long run, Janie and Tom's marriage will survive the differences between them.
Either:
Decide how you think Janie and Tom's relationship will develop and write a short follow-up story that is set some years later and shows the reader what has happened to the couple's feelings for each other since they left the 'Little Palace'.
Or:
Write about times when differences of opinion or personality have put a strain on close friendships of your own. Have such differences completely ruined any of these relationships or do you normally find some way of coming to terms with them?

2   Describe the feelings you imagine you would have if you were about to move away from your present home, or those you remember actually having at such a time. You may like to write this as a poem.

3   Janie obviously does not much care for her Bridge Street neighbours. Write about some of your own neighbours, so that the reader comes to see them as an interesting and varied collection of individuals and to understand just how well or badly you get on with them.

11 WHAT'RE YOU DRINKING?

ALCOHOL FACT SHEET

WHAT IS ALCOHOL

Alcoholic drinks consist mainly of water and ethyl alcohol (or 'ethanol'), produced by the fermentation of fruits, vegetables or grain. The following drinks contain roughly the same amount of alcohol and are counted as *one unit*:

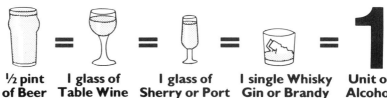

| ½ pint of Beer | 1 glass of Table Wine | 1 glass of Sherry or Port | 1 single Whisky Gin or Brandy | Unit of Alcohol |

THE LAW AND ALCOHOL

It is illegal:

- to give alcohol to a child under five.
- for anyone under fourteen to be in a bar.
- for anyone under eighteen to buy or consume alcohol in a bar or work there.
- to be drunk in a public place, including licenced premises.
- to drive with more than 80 mg of alcohol in every 100 ml of blood. A male of average build will exceed this limit after 2½ pints of beer.

ALCOHOL AND THE BODY

- Alcohol enters the blood through the stomach and intestines. The greater the blood/alcohol concentration (the 'BAC'), the greater will be the effect.
- The BAC depends not only on the number of units drunk but also on the drinker's sex and weight, how fast the drinks are taken and how much food the stomach contains. For example, because women have less body fluid than men to dilute alcohol, what they drink produces a higher BAC.
- The liver removes about 1 unit of alcohol from the blood each hour. So it takes roughly 8 hours to remove 4 pints of beer. It is not true that black coffee, a cold shower or fresh air will speed the sobering-up process.
- One pint of beer can supply as many calories as 6 slices of bread but it is nutritionally worthless since it provides practically no protein or vitamins.

THE SHORT TERM EFFECTS OF DRINKING

- After 3 or 4 units most people feel less inhibited. The emotional reactions range from jovial to aggressive and mental and physical functioning is less efficient.
- After another 3 or 4 units, drinkers generally become

unco-ordinated and slur their words; emotional reactions can be highly exaggerated and unpredictable.

- More drinks will result in staggering, double vision and loss of balance, followed by unconsciousness.

THE SHORT-TERM HAZARDS

- Since just a few drinks impair concentration and co-ordination, the commonest hazard is accidental injury, often from falling or traffic accidents. About a third of drivers and a quarter of all adult pedestrians killed in road accidents have BACs above the legal limit.
- Becoming more emotional and less inhibited can result in violent, criminal or sexually irresponsible behaviour.
- Death through overdose is possible, but is usually prevented when nausea, vomiting or stupor puts a stop to further consumption. Deaths also occur from choking on vomit whilst unconscious.

THE HAZARDS OF LONG-TERM USE

- Regular heavy drinking can lead to overweight; and − since the drinker often goes without proper meals − to protein and vitamin deficiencies.
- It increases the likelihood of ulcers, liver diseases, cancers, heart disorders, infertility and brain damage.
- Babies of women who drank heavily during pregnancy may be born under-weight with withdrawal symptoms and physical and mental abnormalities.
- The drinker may become heavily dependent on alcohol ('alcoholic'), and sudden withdrawal will produce sweating, anxiety, trembling and delirium (the 'DTs') − sometimes convulsions, coma and death.
- Excessive drinking commonly causes or aggravates family, work, personal and financial problems, often leading to family breakdown, or to repeated violence and other forms of crime associated with loss of self-control.

ALCOHOL AND OTHER DRUGS

- Alcohol interacts with many other drugs to produce a stronger effect. With tranquillisers, stimulants and barbiturates it is particularly dangerous − sometimes fatal.
- People who both drink and smoke are at extra risk because alcohol enhances the action of the cancer-producing agents in cigarette smoke.

RECOMMENDED DRINKING LIMITS

- Doctors advise no more than 14 units a week for women, and no more than 21 units for men. Because they are generally smaller, young people should drink less than this.
- To allow the liver and other organs time to recover, two alcohol-free days a week are recommended.

Information provided by Alcohol Concern and The Institute for the Study of Drug Dependence

THE EFFECTS OF ALCOHOL ON ADULT BEHAVIOUR

Number of drinks	Blood alcohol content (mg/100ml)		Usual effect on persons of average build
1 pint of beer or 2 glasses of wine or a double whisky	**30**		increasing likelihood of having an accident
1.5 pints beer or 3 whiskies or half a (75cl) bottle of wine	**50**		increasing cheerfulness, impaired judgement and loosening of inhibitions
2.5 pints of beer or 5 whiskies or 5 glasses of wine	**80**		loss of driving licence if caught
5 pints of beer or 10 whiskies or 1 litre of wine	**150**		loss of self control; quarrelsomeness; exuberance; slurred speech
6 pints of beer or half a bottle of spirits or 2 (75cl) bottles of wine	**200**		stagger; double vision; loss of memory
0.75 bottle of spirits 1 bottle of spirits	**400** **500** **600**		oblivion; sleepiness; coma death possible death certain

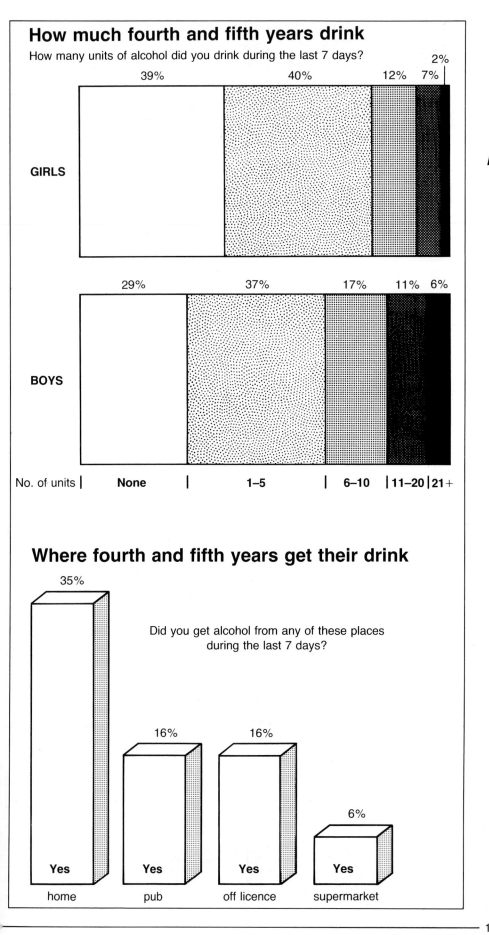

How much fourth and fifth years drink

How many units of alcohol did you drink during the last 7 days?

GIRLS

| 39% | 40% | 12% | 7% | 2% |

BOYS

| 29% | 37% | 17% | 11% | 6% |

No. of units | None | 1–5 | 6–10 | 11–20 | 21+

Where fourth and fifth years get their drink

Did you get alcohol from any of these places during the last 7 days?

35%
Yes
home

16%
Yes
pub

16%
Yes
off licence

6%
Yes
supermarket

YOUNG PEOPLE AND ALCOHOL:
some statistics

THE MAN INSIDE

His mother took him, shaped his seed
Through nine fulfilling months, then watched
Him grow into himself with a speed
That astonished her. She was touched
When he did her credit, alarmed
When he wandered, afraid he might be harmed.

But he could fend for himself, he told
Her. Although his dad had died
When he was only four years old
His young maturity seemed to glow inside.
Running or swimming or jumping a fence
He simply shone with commonsense.

He left her lonely in his teens,
He passed from her hands to university;
His letters home had undertones
That hinted as some dark adversity.
Still, he was young, she mused:
Too fine to let his body be abused.

Away from home, with clever friends,
He took to drinking every night.
He was a sop who soaked up trends,
A chameleon turning red and bright.
In the mornings he pissed and yawned,
Then back to bed before the day had dawned.

He passed out with a second-class degree
And went to work selling deathly policies;
He took a wife for captive company,
Lovingly exposed all her fallacies.
He toyed with the idea of revolution;
His mind was settled in a strong solution.

His policies suffered, his driving got worse
He became too befuddled to think;
He would drive distracted with a quiet curse
Searching for bars where he could still buy drink.
One day the sound of crunching metal
Smashed the man inside the bottle.

ALAN BOLD

1   Use information from the Alcohol Fact Sheet to reply to these comments:
    As far as the law on alcohol goes, you can do what you like in your own home.
    It's an hour since my last drink, so I'm okay to drive.
    Beer is a meal in itself so I never bother eating before I go to the pub.
    People who drink too much are hurting nobody but themselves.

2   Study the statistics on page 73. Do they give us reasons to be worried about young people and alcohol? Refer to specific figures in your answer.

3   Why, when the man in Alan Bold's poem, *The Man Inside,* left for university, did people feel he was going to make a success of his life?

4   In what ways had the man failed to live up to these high expectations by the time he died?

Answer one of the following:

Response

1   You have been asked to give a short talk to the first year, warning them of the dangers of alcohol.
    Base your talk on the Alcohol Fact Sheet and the statistics, but remember that your audience will be much less mature than you. They must be able to understand your information easily at one hearing, and the way you present it must make a strong impression on them, so simply stringing together sentences from the fact sheet would not make a good talk.

2   Produce a two-sided leaflet that could be used as part of a sensible-drinking campaign targeted at 13- to 16-year-olds. Side one should be an eye-catching design that captures the readers' attention and makes them want to turn to side two; there they will find facts about the hazards of alcohol abuse and what counts as safe drinking.
    You should take most of your information from the Alcohol Fact Sheet and the statistics, but add any ideas of your own that might help get the message across. Before you begin, see page 128 for suggestions on how to write leaflets of this kind.

3   Suppose that you are the mother mentioned in *The Man Inside* and that after your son's death, you come across the poem. Reading it brings back a flood of memories and feelings about your son, some happy, some, of course, very sad. Write down these reactions to the poem, basing your work on the facts Alan Bold provides, but adding ideas of your own.

Your Writing

Answer one of the following:

1 Drinking is an expensive pastime and can be a very dangerous one, as the Alcohol Fact Sheet shows. So why are so many people drawn to it? And ought not the law to treat alcohol as strictly as it does other dangerous substances, like heroin?

   What are your views on these questions and any others you think are raised by the growing problem of alcohol misuse?

2 Referring to the short-term hazards of alcohol, the fact sheet says:

   Becoming more emotional and less inhibited can result in violent, criminal or sexually irresponsible behaviour.

   Think of the human suffering that lies behind this sentence, then write a true or imaginary story, or poem, that will bring home to readers the misery a session of heavy drinking can cause.

3 The statistics on young people's drinking habits on page 73 are typical of the many surveys of behaviour and opinions that are published each year and which can be so useful in helping us understand what is happening in our society.

   Conduct your own survey among members of the class, or a larger group, on a topic that interests you. These are the sort of subjects you might choose:
   how they spend their leisure time,
   how much freedom their parents or guardians allow them,
   what their attitudes are towards school,
   how much money they are given or earn a week and what they do with it,
   what views they have on an issue like blood sports, abortion or drugs.

   Plan your questions carefully and, as far as possible, offer a limited choice of responses so that you can assess the answers more easily. When you have finished the survey, present the results in a clear and lively way. The statistics on page 73 and elsewhere in the book show how this can be done. Then comment on your survey, explaining why you chose the particular topic and drawing the reader's attention to points worth noting in your findings.

Alan Paton was a white South African whose writing dealt largely with the problems faced by non-whites in his country. One such problem is the break-up of old African communities as their young people flock to the towns in search of work; and another — the subject of this short story — is the lawlessness, violence and despair into which town-dwellers can sink when they leave behind them the traditional village discipline and values.

12 THE WASTE LAND

The moment that the bus moved on he knew he was in danger, for by the lights of it he saw the figures of the young men waiting under the tree. That was the thing feared by all, to be waited for by the young men. It was a thing he had talked about, now he was to see it for himself.

It was too late to run after the bus; it went down the dark street like an island of safety in a sea of perils. Though he had known of his danger only for a second, his mouth was already dry, his heart was pounding in his breast, something within him was crying out in protest against the coming event.

His wages were in his purse, he could feel them weighing heavily against his thigh. That was what they wanted from him. Nothing counted against that. His wife could be made a widow, his children made fatherless, nothing counted against that. Mercy was the unknown word.

While he stood there irresolute he heard the young men walking towards him, not only from the side where he had seen them, but from the other also. They did not speak, their intention was unspeakable. The sound of their feet came on the wind to him. The place was well chosen, for behind him was the high wall of the convent, and the barred door that would not open before a man was dead. On the other side of the road was the waste land, full of wire and iron and the bodies of old cars. It was his only hope, and he moved towards it; as he did so he knew from the whistle that the young men were there too.

His fear was great and instant, and the smell of it went from his body to his nostrils. At that very moment one of them spoke, giving directions. So trapped was he that he was filled suddenly with strength and anger, and he ran towards the waste land swinging his heavy stick. In the darkness a form loomed up at him, and he swung at it, and heard it give a cry of pain. Then he plunged blindly into the wilderness of wire and iron and the bodies of old cars.

Something caught him by the leg, and he brought his stick crashing down on it, but it was no man, only some knife-edged piece of iron. He was sobbing and out of breath, but he pushed on into the waste, while behind him they pushed on also, knocking against the old iron bodies and kicking against tins and buckets. He fell into some grotesque shape of wire; it was barbed and tore at his clothes and flesh. Then it held him, so that it seemed to him that death must be near, and having no other hope, he cried out, 'Help me, help me!' in what should have been a great voice but was voiceless and gasping. He tore at the wire, and it tore at him too, ripping his face and his hands.

Then suddenly he was free. He saw the bus returning, and he cried out again in the great voiceless voice, 'Help me, help me!' Against the lights of it he could plainly see the form of one of the young men. Death was near him, and for a moment he was filled with the injustice of life, that could end thus for one who had always been hard-working and law-abiding. He lifted the heavy stick and brought it down on the head of his pursuer, so that the man crumpled to the ground, moaning and groaning as though life had been unjust to him also.

Then he turned and began to run again, but ran first into the side of an old lorry which sent him reeling. He lay there for a moment expecting the blow that would end him, but even then his wits came back to him, and he turned over twice and was under the lorry. His very entrails seemed to be coming out his mouth, and his lips could taste sweat and blood. His heart was like a wild thing in his breast, and seemed to lift his whole body each time that it beat. He tried to calm it down, thinking it might be heard, and tried to

control the noise of his gasping breath, but he could not do either of these things.

Then suddenly against the dark sky he saw two of the young men. He thought they must hear him; but they themselves were gasping like drowned men, and their speech came by fits and starts.

Then one of them said, 'Do you hear?'

They were silent except for their gasping, listening. And he listened also, but could hear nothing but his own exhausted heart.

'I heard a man . . . running . . . on the road,' said one. 'He's got away . . . let's go.'

Then some more of the young men came up, gasping and cursing the man who had got away.

'Freddy,' said one, 'your father's got away.'

But there was no reply.

'Where's Freddy?' one asked.

One said, 'Quiet!' Then he called in a loud voice, 'Freddy.'

But there was still no reply.

'Let's go,' he said.

They moved off slowly and carefully, then one of them stopped.

'We are saved,' he said. 'Here is the man.'

He knelt down on the ground, and then fell to cursing.

'There's no money here,' he said.

One of them lit a match, and in the small light of it the man under the lorry saw him fall back.

'It's Freddy,' one said. 'He's dead.'

Then the one who had said 'Quiet' spoke again.

'Lift him up,' he said. 'Put him under the lorry.'

The man under the lorry heard them struggling with the body of the dead young man, and he turned once, twice, deeper into his hiding place. The young men lifted the body and swung it under the lorry so that it touched him. Then he heard them moving away, not speaking, slowly and quietly, making an occasional sound against some obstruction in the waste.

He turned on his side, so that he would not need to touch the body of the young man. He buried his face in his arms, and said to himself in the idiom of his own language, 'People, arise! The world is dead.' Then he arose himself, and went heavily out of the waste land.

ALAN PATON

THUG

School began it.
There he felt
the tongue's salt lash
raising a welt

on a child's heart.
Ten years ruled
by violence left him
thoroughly schooled,

nor did he fail
to understand
the blow of the
headmaster's hand.

That hand his hand
round the cosh curled.
What rules the classroom
rocks the world.

RAYMOND GARLICK

Understanding

1 We are given a strong impression of the man's fear in the first half of the story. What details on pages 77 and 78 show us how frightened he is?

2 How does Paton convince us that the man's attackers are not just a few rowdy boys up to mischief but an extremely dangerous gang of young criminals?

3 Read the last paragraph carefully. How would you describe and explain the effect this incident has had on the man?

4 Often the setting, the physical surroundings, in which a story takes place has been carefully chosen by the author. Paton calls his story *The Waste Land* so he must have thought that *where* the incident happened was important. Describe this setting in detail and then suggest reasons why the author chose it.

5 The meaning of the poem *Thug* is summed up in the last two lines: 'What rules the classroom rocks the world.' Explain what Raymond Garlick means by this and how he has tried to show it is true earlier in the poem.

Response

Answer one of the following:

1 Continue Alan Paton's story by writing about the man's return home and how he breaks the news to the rest of the family. We see from the passage that he is devastated by what has happened. This should be clear from your part of the story too. How the family react to what he tells them is for you to decide.

2 Write a report of this incident as it might appear in a newspaper the next day. Imagine that you have interviewed the man in the story and include some of his comments in your article. Before you begin, look at page 121. The suggestions there on writing newspaper reports will help you get the most interest out of the story.

3 Suppose you are the thug in Raymond Garlick's poem. Help us to understand what made you the way you are by explaining important lines in the poem and giving us examples of what the poet is referring to in your school life.

Answer one of the following:

1 Alan Paton tells us that when Freddy was knocked to the ground, he groaned 'as though life had been unjust to him too'. This makes us wonder how Freddy came to be involved in the attempted robbery, especially if he knew who the victim would be.

   Think carefully about these questions and then write the lead-up to the crime in a story which ends where Alan Paton's begins.

2 Write about a time when you have been frightened. You will probably never have been through an event as terrifying as the one Paton describes, but much more ordinary occasions can be scaring, for example, a visit to the dentist, having to speak in public, walking home alone at night or starting a new school.

   Try to show the reader exactly how you were feeling. Think about how the bodily reactions of the man in the passage and the way he behaved and spoke all showed how frightened he was.

3 Being betrayed by someone close to you is a dreadful experience. Take this as the theme for a piece of writing.

   You could write about times when you felt badly let down by people you trusted or tell a true or imaginary story about one particular betrayal.

13
HOME
TRUTHS?

These opinions on teenagers are taken from interviews with parents in Mary McCormack's book *The Generation Gap*.

Ron, father of Karen (14) and Andrew (13)

To me, the worst thing about teenagers is this anti-everything attitude. You know − 'What a dump', when you take them somewhere. 'What a Wally' for everyone over 30 − or even another teenager who dresses differently. Perpetual scorn and boredom with everything. They don't want to go anywhere or do anything. If you suggest a drive in the country, they look at you as if you're mad. Maybe it's because they've seen it all now by the time they start school − if not first-hand, then on television.

The thing that amazes me is the total lack of respect they have for adults. There's no way my generation would have stood up to an adult and rubbished what they were saying. We'd have got a sharp clout across the ear.

The young girls are even harder to understand than boys. Your daughter can turn overnight into a total stranger. Suddenly the pretty little girl is putting warpaint on her face, dyeing her hair a funny colour and wearing the most awful clothes − by the time she is thirteen. My daughter is a clever, pretty girl, who takes off her smart school uniform and deliberately turns herself into the biggest mess you ever laid eyes on. If you try to advise her, she says you have no idea what's fashionable. If you refuse to let her out looking like that, there's rows and days of sulking.

Tarted up, she can look years older. I realise you can't lock them up, but I don't think a girl under 16 should be going out alone with a boy, even a lad her own age. I know what young lads are like. I don't believe in abortion. And giving a girl of 14 or 15 the pill is just obscene. It's like neutering a cat. 'Take one of these daily and forget about morals and decency'. That is opting out of parental responsibility.

The reason young people behave so badly is precisely *because* so many parents shrug their shoulders and give in. You don't have to. You can put your foot down firmly, early, and keep it there. I mean, it's for their good; it's because you want the best for them. Sooner or later they'll realise that.

Mary, mother of Tina (14) and Wayne (13)

Their relationships with the opposite sex are serious — and that's one of the biggest worries. Tina goes out in a foursome — with her friend and their boyfriends — and they come back as a foursome. But I know they split into twosomes while they are out.

Of course sex is thrown at them from all sides — films, newspapers, television. Boy-friends were a long way from my mind at Tina's age. Pop stars pinned on the bedroom wall was the nearest I got.

I try to censor what they see. I won't have a video because I know the sort of films they can get — not hard porn or anything, just suggestive modern films. I try not to let them see anything I don't like the sound of.

Ray is married to Mary

You have to come down firmly and say, 'That is it, not a minute later.' I don't think they believe how you worry. From the moment your child goes out, there's a little nagging worry at the back of your mind. Every minute after the time they are supposed to be in that worry builds up. By the time they get in you're ready to explode so what they see is anger and bad temper, not your fear for them.

Maureen has three teenage sons

Darren, the 17-year-old, he drives me mad. He's so dirty, you see. It's disgusting. You can't get him to have a bath. When he washes, it's a case of wiping a cloth round his neck, leaving a trail in the grime.

Julie has one teenage daughter and two sons

Debbie comes and goes as she pleases. Well, she's 19 now. From her mid-teens it was more a case of her telling us what time she would be home than us telling her when to come in. She trained us to it. I think you have to lower your standards, accept a different set of standards from those you were brought up on.

Denise, mother of Sharon (15), Teresa (14) and a younger daughter

We can watch television together and if there's something – well, questionable, we can talk about it. I know a 13-year-old boy who cannot see a couple kissing on the screen without going beetroot with embarrassment. What sort of attitude is he going to grow up with?

I find television is a very good starting-point. If there is some item on VD or something, I'll say to the girls, 'Do you know what that means?' If not, I tell them.

The only thing that irritates me is their casual assumption that money grows on trees. They'll ask for a computer for a birthday present or a video-recorder. All I ever got was some sweets or a couple of oranges or a doll if I was really lucky. But all their friends have them, so you go without yourself so they won't be different.

Janet, mother of Mandy (13) and Beth (14)

I won't have newspapers in the house, except the evening paper, because of the rubbish that is in them; nor are Beth and Mandy allowed to watch television late at night. They go to bed – or at least up to their rooms – at 9 o'clock. Partly for their own benefit and partly, I'll be honest, because that is the only time in the day Alan and I get together. I think it's very important to get a bit of time together as a couple.

Alan is married to Janet

Bringing up a girl is more worrying than having a boy. There's always this worry over sexual things. It's not an equal world. Girls get left with the consequences, so you are stricter on them.

Just the same, I don't agree with my wife about everything. If Beth came to me and said, tomorrow, that she wanted to go on the pill, I'd agree. I'd think that the fact that she'd thought about it and got the confidence to approach me, meant that she was mature enough.

Roger, father of Amy (14) and three younger children

Parents feel guilty about not being able to chat matily to their teenagers about sex, but I wonder if it isn't part of the taboo imposed by nature and maybe a good thing. Perhaps we are meant to find it a bit embarrassing. Very few young people actually want to hear that sort of information from their parents. It's as embarrassing for them as for us.

We don't have a television set on principle. We didn't want them exposed to violence and blatant sex prematurely and it wastes so much time. It has caused me some heart-searching. I am aware of the effect being different can have on an adolescent among their friends.

Paul is the father of three older teenagers, two boys and a girl

I like to know where my kids are and what they are up to. But you have no way of knowing, do you? What's Tom (19) up to when he goes out at 10 p.m. and doesn't get home till 3 a.m.? He certainly never volunteers the information. He does treat the house like a hotel and that annoys me. I don't know why exactly. Maybe it's envy. I have to say where I'm going and get home at a reasonable hour or there will be rows with my wife.

Their lack of activity drives me mad, the way they can sit around for hours without any apparent feeling of boredom or guilt. You'd think the least they could do is help in the house and keep their rooms tidy, without having to be nagged continually.

Understanding

1 Many of the complaints these fathers and mothers make are aimed more at their children's *attitudes* than at anything particularly dreadful in their behaviour. Describe fully *four* of the attitudes they object to.

2 As we might expect, the parents do not see eye to eye on all questions concerning the way children should be brought up. What are the matters on which they disagree?

3 It is often said that parents take a harder line with their teenage daughters than they do with their sons. Do the extracts show this is true and help to explain why there is a difference in attitude? In your answer, you should refer closely to actual comments made by the parents.

Response

Answer one of the following:

1 How sympathetic are you to the criticisms made in the extracts? Do you think any of them are justified? Are there any you think unreasonable? Limit yourself to discussing three or four of the criticisms and give clear reasons for your own opinions.

2 Ron, the first to speak, has the most to say about parenthood and the problems he faces with his son and daughter. His remarks give us a clear idea of the likely tensions and arguments in his family.

Describe what you think would be a typical scene involving Ron and his two children, presenting your work either as a short story or in the form of a play. You will find suggestions on how to write a play on pages 124 and 125.

3 Imagine that three or four of the teenagers named in the extracts, from different families, appear together on a television programme called *Family Matters*. The programme is a chaired discussion in which young people air their views on family life: the most common causes of friction, the attitudes of their parents they most dislike, where they admit they themselves may be at fault, and so on.

Write the script of five minutes or so of the programme, basing your work closely on information in the extracts. Pages 124 to 125 will help you set out your script in the right way.

Remember, this is a discussion, not simply a question and answer session. The teenagers are exchanging experiences and opinions and will not always find themselves in agreement.

Answer one of the following:

1   Write about your experiences with your own parents or the people with whom you live, concentrating on how your relationships with them have changed as you have got older and the problems, if any, that have arisen. You may want to relate some of the comments made by the parents in the passage to your own case.

2   These statements are taken from the passage:
    'Your daughter can turn overnight into a total stranger.'
    'Their relationships with the opposite sex are serious — and that's one of the biggest worries.'
    'What they see is anger and bad temper, not your fear for them.'
    'He does treat the house like a hotel and that annoys me. I don't know why exactly. Maybe it's envy.'

    Using ideas suggested to you by one or more of these remarks, write a poem or short story that deals in a sensitive way with the feelings on both sides in the parent/child relationship.

3   Half the parents quoted in the passage have strong views concerning television. They obviously consider it an important influence in the home, though not necessarily a good one. What, in your opinion, does television contribute to our lives and in what ways might we be better off without it?

14 REMOTE

Around about the end of each month she would write a letter, but because it was December she used an old Christmas card, which she found at the bottom of the biscuit tin among her pension books. She stood dressed in her outdoor clothes on tiptoe at the bedroom window waiting for the bird-watcher's Land Rover to come over the top of the hill two miles away. When she saw it she dashed, slamming the door after her and running in her stiff-legged fashion down the lane on to the road. Her aim was to be walking, breathing normally, when the Land Rover would indicate and stop in the middle of the one-track road.

'Can I give you a lift?'

'Aye.'

She walked round the front of the shuddering engine and climbed up to sit on the split seat. Mushroom-coloured foam bulged from its crack. More often than not she had to kick things aside to make room for her feet. It was not the lift she would have chosen but it was all there was. He shoved the wobbling stick through the gears and she had to shout — each month the same thing.

'Where are you for?'

'The far side.'

'I'm always lucky to catch you.'

He dressed like one of those hitch-hikers, green khaki jacket, cord trousers and laced-up mountain boots. His hair was long and unwashed and his beard divided into points like the teats of a goat.

'Are you going as far as the town this time?'

'Yes.'

'Will you drop me off?'

'Sure. Christmas shopping?'

'Aye, that'll be right.'

The road spun past, humping and squirming over peat bogs, the single track bulging at passing points — points which were marked by tall black and white posts to make them stand out against the landscape. Occasionally in the bog there were incisions, a black-brown colour, herring-boned with scars where peat had been cut.

'How's the birds doing?' she shouted.

'Fine. I've never had so many as this year.'

His accent was English and it surprised her that he had blackheads dotting his cheekbones and dirty hands.

'Twenty-two nesting pairs — so far.'

'That's nice.'

'Compared to sixteen last year.'

'What are they?'

He said what they were but she couldn't hear him properly. They joined the main road and were silent for a while. Then rounding a corner the bird-man suddenly applied the brakes. Two cars, facing in opposite directions, sat in the middle of the road, their drivers having a conversation. The bird-man muttered and steered round them, the Land Rover tilting as it mounted the verge.

'I'd like to see them try that in Birmingham.'

'Is that where you're from?'

He nodded.

'Why did you come to the island?'

'The birds.'

He smiled and pointed to an open packet of Polo mints on the dashboard. She lifted them and saw that the top sweet was soiled, the relief letters almost black. She prised it out and gave it to him. The white one beneath she put in her mouth.

'Thanks,' she said.

'You born on the island?'

'City born and bred.' She snorted. 'I was lured here by a man forty-two years ago.'

'I never see him around.'

'I'm not surprised. He's dead this long time.' She cracked the ring of mint between her teeth.

'I'm sorry.'

She chased the two crescents of mint around her tongue.

'What did he do?'

'He drowned himself. In the loch.'

'I'm sorry, I didn't mean that.'

'On Christmas Day. He went mad in the skull — away with the fairies.'

There was a long pause in which he said again that he was sorry. Then he said, 'What I meant was — what did he do for a living?'

'What does it matter now?'

The bird-man shook his head and concentrated on the road ahead.

'He was a shepherd,' she said. Then a little later, 'He was the driver. There should always be one in the house who can drive.'

He let her off at the centre of the village and she had to walk the steep hill to the Post Office. She breathed through her mouth and took a rest halfway up, holding on to a small railing. Distances grew with age.

Inside she passed over her pension book, got her money and bought a first-class stamp. She waited until she was outside before she took the letter from her bag. She licked the stamp, stuck it on the envelope and dropped it in the letter box. Walking down the hill was easier.

She went to the Co-op to buy sugar and tea and porridge. The shop was strung with skimpy tinselled decorations and the music they were playing was Christmas hits — 'Rudolf' and 'I saw Mammy Kissing Santa Claus'. She only had a brief word with Elizabeth at the check-out because of the queue behind her. In the butcher's she bought herself a pork chop and some bacon. His bacon lasted longer than the packet stuff.

When she had her shopping finished she wondered what to do to pass the time. She could visit young Mary but if she did she would have to talk. Not having enough things to say she felt

awkward listening to the tick of the clock and the distant cries of sea birds. Chat was a thing you got out of the habit of when you were on your own all the time and, besides, Mary was shy. Instead she decided to buy a cup of tea in the cafe. And treat herself to an almond bun. She sat near the window where she could look out for the post van.

The cafe was warm and it, too, was decorated. Each time the door opened the hanging fronds of tinsel fluttered. On a tape somewhere carols were playing. Two children, sitting with their mother, were playing with a new toy car on the table-top. The cellophane wrapping had been discarded on the floor. They both imitated engine noises although only one of them was pushing it round the plates. The other sat impatiently waiting for his turn.

She looked away from them and stared into her tea. When they dredged him up on Boxing Day he had two car batteries tied to his wrists. He was nothing if not thorough. One of them had been taken from his own van parked by the loch shore and the thing had to be towed to the garage. If he had been a drinking man he could have been out getting drunk or fallen into bad company. But there was only the black depression. All that day the radio had been on to get rid of the dread.

When 'Silent Night' came on the tape and the children started to squabble over whose turn it was she did not wait to finish her tea but walked slowly to the edge of the village with her bag of shopping, now and again pausing to look over her shoulder. The scarlet of the post van caught her eye and she stood on the verge with her arm out. When she saw it was Stuart driving she smiled. He stopped the van and she ducked down to look in the window.

'Anything for me today?'

He leaned across to the basket of mail which occupied the passenger seat position and began to rummage through the bundles of letters and cards held together with elastic bands.

'This job would be all right if it wasn't for bloody Christmas.' He paused at her single letter. 'Aye, there's just one.'

'Oh, good. You might as well run me up, seeing as you're going that way.'

He sighed and looked over his shoulder at a row of houses.

'Wait for me round the corner.'

She nodded and walked on ahead while he made some deliveries. The lay-by was out of sight of the houses and she set her bag down to wait. Stuart seemed to take a long time. She looked down at the loch in the growing dark. The geese were returning for the night, filling the air with their squawking. They sounded like a dance-hall full of people laughing and enjoying themselves, heard from a distance on the night wind.

BERNARD MAC LAVERTY

1 What do we learn about the woman's husband from the story?

2 At which points in the story does the woman find herself thinking about her husband? What is it that triggers off her memory of him at these particular times?

3 Getting in and out of town is a problem for the woman. How does she deal with it?

4 Does any of the information we are given about the woman and about the island itself suggest what might have been the reasons she did not go back to the mainland after her husband's death?

5 A good writer notices details, often small, familiar ones the rest of us would pass over, and finds exactly the right words to describe them. For example, on page 90 Bernard Mac Laverty mentions the Land Rover's 'shuddering engine', its 'wobbling' gear stick and the way 'mushroom-coloured foam bulged' from cracks in the seat. List four or five other examples of this sort of attention to detail, underlining any words you think are especially well chosen.

6 Can you think of reasons why Bernard Mac Laverty called his story 'Remote'?

Answer one of the following:

1 How readers react to the woman in Mac Laverty's story could be quite complicated — for example, they might be generally very sorry for her but also find her amusing or even annoying at times.

What are your own feelings about the woman? Explain clearly what it is about her that makes you feel this way.

2 Imagine that later the two men who appear in this story, Stuart and the bird-watcher, meet socially, perhaps in the pub. They discover they have both given the woman a lift during the day and go on to talk about her and the impressions they have of her.

Write this part of their conversation, setting it out as a play if you wish. You should base your work on the facts the author gives, but you could add interest to the conversation by making the men differ in the opinions they have of the woman. You will find suggestions on how to write a play on pages 124 to 125.

3 If the woman were a relative of yours, you would probably be concerned about her living alone in such a remote spot.

Write her a letter tactfully suggesting she should consider moving back to a town on the mainland. You will need to use arguments to persuade her. Some of these arguments should be based on what you know about her particular situation, others could be more general arguments you think might convince any elderly person it is better to live in a town.

Before you begin your letter, read the suggestions on page 122.

Your writing

Answer one of the following:

1 Bernard Mac Laverty does not tell us directly how the woman feels about her life now she is alone or how she felt when her husband died. Nor does he explain what she means by 'I was lured here by a man forty-two years ago.'

Write three or four entries which she might have made in her diary at different times during the last forty-two years and which help the reader understand the way her feelings have changed since she arrived on the island.

2 The story gives us a good idea of what it is like living in a remote country area. Write a piece of description, a poem perhaps, which creates an equally strong impression of city life.

3 We know that when people become old their lives can be very difficult, but is this actually borne out in your own experience of the elderly? You may write about several old people you have known or, if you prefer, concentrate on just one individual.

SHOULD THIS RABBIT BE USED IN EXPERIMENTS?

In laboratory tests, rabbits like this have chemicals dripped into their eyes to measure how much pain they feel. Some people say it's cruel to inflict suffering on helpless animals, others that it's the only way to make medical advances. So should these experiments continue?

YES

MARGARET FRANKLIN

*General Secretary
of the
Research Defence
Society*

★ A great deal of public concern was shown for three-year-old Ben Hardwick after the BBC's *That's Life* programme took up his case. After two transplants, Ben died in 1985.

★ Many babies were born misformed in the 1960s after their mothers took this drug during their pregnancies.

Isn't it marvellous when lives are saved thanks to modern surgery?

With transplants, those in pain and suffering can return to a normal life. Because of vaccines, killer diseases like diphtheria, polio, smallpox and tuberculosis have been beaten. Hip joint replacements can transform a cripple to an active person, while insulin saves diabetics from certain death.

All this has been made possible because of experiments on animals. Without vivisection, little Ben Hardwick, who captured the nation's heart when he needed a liver transplant, could not have had an operation at all.* But there wasn't one word in all the publicity that followed about scientists who pioneered the treatment – using trials on animals.

It is fashionable today to criticise modern drugs and the ways we develop them, but people forget the countless millions of lives that have been saved by them.

And of course, animals themselves can benefit from the experiments. Remember Sefton, the cavalry horse badly injured in an IRA bomb blast? He was brought back to good health using techniques tested by vivisectors who do a lot of work to help veterinary surgery. They've even developed vital vaccines which prevent diseases like cat flu and distemper.

What people don't understand is that some animal experiments are required by law. For our own protection, drugs must be tested to check they are safe before they're used by human beings.

One tragic case where a drug was not tested thoroughly on animals was, of course, thalidomide.* And we all know the heart-breaking results that caused. Animals are the only models we have for human beings. They aren't ideal, but they are the best we've got.

You see, a drug has to be tested on an entire body system. Carrying out the same tests on some tissue in a dish simply doesn't give accurate results. That's why animal experiments are so important.

Certainly, we are very keen to see alternative methods researched and developed, and many of our members have been involved in this work. It's very expensive to use animals continually, so there's every incentive to find other ways of carrying out tests. And anyway, scientists must use an alternative by law wherever possible. There has been a steady reduction in the number of animals used during the past decade.

In any case, it's rats and mice that make up the vast majority of all the animals tested. And we kill those animals at home ourselves. Sometimes it's necessary to use larger animals, like cats, dogs and rabbits, but they only account for a tiny proportion of animals used.

Scientists aren't sadists. Everything is done to keep the animal undergoing experiments comfortable and happy. Drugs are given to animals after operations to help recovery as they would be to human beings. Animals suffering too much pain are killed humanely. But most tests involve simply taking a blood sample or giving an innoculation. If the animal is not being well cared for, it will not produce the all-important results.

Many people object to animals being used in tests in the manufacture of cosmetics. But it's not just eye shadow and mascara which are tested on animals. It's soap, detergents and baby shampoo, things we use every day which must be safe.

All experiments are strictly controlled by the government. The Home Office is informed of all trials and every detail of a project must be explained before permission is given for the experiment. For those who break the rules, the penalties are severe.

If we are ever going to cure cancer, and conquer AIDS, vivisection must be allowed to continue for the foreseeable future.

Vivisection doesn't work. Quite simply, the results of animal experiments cannot be applied successfully to human beings – history has proved it. The introduction of blood transfusions was delayed for more than 200 years by the misleading results from animal experiments.

Chloroform, a useful anaesthetic in people, actually kills dogs, while morphine, often used as a tranquilliser, sparks wild excitement in cats and mice. And Flory, the man who purified penicillin, always said it was a lucky chance he didn't test it on guinea pigs as it kills them.

So, you see, it is nonsense to suggest that experiments are necessary to make strides forward. They can actually be dangerous in producing misleading results.

The simple fact is animals aren't like us: they suffer from different diseases – and diseases they're given that are made in a laboratory aren't the same as the real world.

The inhumanity to animals is appalling. In one test, an animal, usually a rabbit, has a chemical product such as hairspray or an industrial cleaner, dripped into its eye to see how much it irritates it. No pain relief is given. It goes on for up to seven days while scientists slowly study the

JAN CREAMER

General Secretary of the National Anti-Vivisection Society

ulceration, bleeding and swelling. We think it's outrageous to inflict such suffering. What's worse is that the test doesn't prove very much as a rabbit's eye is different to a human's.

The other disgraceful waste of life is the 'safety' test when animals are force-fed a substance like weedkiller and detergent to find out how much is needed to kill them. It can last up to 14 days. And what does that prove? Water can be lethal if you pump enough into a creature. You simply overload the system until it collapses. We want to see this kind of useless experimentation banned.

Many advances have been made in medicine without using animals. Contrary to the stories told, insulin, the life-saving drug for diabetics, was purified for use by a chemist without using animals.

Scientists have made us believe that drugs cure so many illnesses, but epidemics of diseases like diphtheria were on the wane before antibiotics came in. It was the leaps ahead in levels of health and hygiene that eradicated them.

In the research to find drugs to cure cancer, much of the testing is done on mice. But mice suffer a different kind of cancer to humans. And the cancers induced in a laboratory grow quite differently from natural cancers − so treatment can have a different effect. The tests cannot be conclusive.

Drugs must go through clinical tests on human beings before they are available to the public anyway. We say that any experiments carried out before that point are completely invalid. It's the reaction in humans that counts, and that alone.

We fund medical research that doesn't torture animals and we've made quite a significant contribution to medical progress, including the bid to understand cot deaths. And we've proved there are viable alternatives. We developed experiments on the human placenta − an ideal substitute for animals − and there are thousands of them thrown away every year.*

* The placenta is the organ in a woman's womb which allows her to feed her baby before it is born; it is discarded after the birth.

More and more young people are coming round to our idea. In fact, our 'Violence Free Science' campaign − run to give students the right to refuse to take part in dissection of animals in classes − has been one of the most successful ever.

Our bid to stop vivisection is based on scientific evidence. We've got plenty of it now.

Experiments on animals are as unproductive as they are inhuman and sickeningly cruel. We think the suffering should end.

Taken from *Woman's Own* magazine

1 That part of the article which appears on page 95 — the photograph, the headline and the seven lines of introduction — has been added by the editor of *Woman's Own*. Do you think both Margaret Franklin and Jan Creamer would be happy with this material? Give clear reasons for your answer.

2 The two writers have very different attitudes towards experiments on animals but they also flatly contradict each other about the facts. For example, Ms Franklin says the experiments must be performed on 'an entire body system', whereas Ms Creamer claims that a human placenta will do just as well. How many more disagreements of a factual nature can you find in the article?

3 Animal experimenters are often thought of as hard, uncaring scientists who lack normal human feelings. How does Ms Franklin try to change this image in the article? Consider not only *what* she says but also *how* she says it.

4 The charge is made against animal campaigners that they rely too much on emotion and refuse to face scientific facts. Is Ms Creamer's approach emotional, scientific or a mixture of the two? In your answer, refer closely to examples of what she writes in the article.

Answer one of the following:

1 Write the script of a discussion you have with whichever of the two writers you find less convincing. Go over her main arguments in turn, raising in a calm, reasonable way any objections you have to them and imagining what she might reply. Some of your objections could be taken from the other half of the article, others might be ideas of your own. (The suggestions on pages 124 and 125 will help you set out your script in the right way.)

2 Your school organises a meeting at which Ms Franklin and Ms Creamer argue their cases in the same way they have done in the *Woman's Own* article. The editor of your school magazine asks you to write an interesting report of the meeting in 200 to 250 words.

   You will not be able to cover everything that was said, so stick to just the main arguments. You will need to be impartial, so although you may have strong opinions on this topic, readers of your report should not be able to tell what they are.

3 Suppose that the campaigners either for or against animal experiments buy space in a national newspaper and run an

advertisement the size of a sheet of A4 paper. Their aim, of course, is to win public support. To do this they need an advertisement that has real impact and presents a few facts and arguments as forcefully as possible.

Design what you think would be a successful advertisement, taking most of your material from the article but adding any ideas of your own which you think will help your case. You will find it useful to read the suggestions on page 128 before you begin.

Your writing

Answer one of the following:

1 The use of animals in experiments is only one of the issues raised by people who campaign for animal rights. They also oppose blood sports, factory farming, hunting or breeding animals for their furs, circuses and other forms of what they see as cruelty to innocent creatures.

   What do you feel on the animal rights question? You may want to limit yourself to just one or two issues, or you may prefer to discuss the topic more generally. Try to give well argued reasons for your views.

2 If you have kept pets, you know that you soon come to see them as important members of the family and interesting characters in their own right.
   Either:
   Write about a pet you have owned, so that the reader gets an accurate impression of its personality and of what it contributes or used to contribute to the life of the family.
   Or:
   Give an account of your household from a pet's point of view, writing as though you are recording the animal's own thoughts. You could try this as a poem if you wish.

3 The article from *Woman's Own* is a good illustration of 'persuasive' writing: the arguments are well stated in a clear, lively way and made more convincing by well chosen examples, and the writers adopt a friendly, reasonable tone that makes us more sympathetic to their views.

   Bearing these points in mind, write a magazine article that sets out to persuade the reader on some subject about which you feel strongly. Capital punishment, single-sex schools, aid to the Third World — these are the sort of topics you could choose.

16
THE
VISITOR

He was odd. Below his grey, felt hat he had an uncertain smile which confused me a little as I somehow got the strange impression that I was making him uncomfortable. He remained silent for a long time. I began to detect something sinister about him.

Suddenly, he said, in an almost apologetic voice, 'You Miss Gladys' son?' There was a faint smell of rum and toothpaste. I nodded. He kept staring at me; his mouth remained slightly open. His eyes were watery, curious and a little sad.

'You want me to call her for you?' I asked.

'What?' He seemed surprised that I was capable of asking a question; or perhaps that I had been daring enough to put one to him. He swallowed, stared at me with even greater curiosity, and then murmured. 'Oh, call her? Yes, yes, do that.'

What a funny man, I thought, as I went to the door.

'Mamma.'

'What?'

'A man out here to see you.'

'A man? Which man that?'

'Don't know him. Never seen him before.'

She got up and peeped through the window. By now I was anxious myself to know who the stranger might be and so I observed her closely as she peered outside at him. She stared and stared. She did not move and seemed petrified by the window. I walked inside and had a mild shock as I saw her expression.

'What happen, Mamma?'

She did not answer. I realised that something was very wrong. I had never known her to be confronted with a situation which she seemed in any way incapable of handling. Not until that moment.

'Mama . . . ?'

'Go an' tell 'im me not here . . . go an' tell 'im . . . no, wait, tell 'im . . . tell 'im me coming.'

Whoever the stranger was I realised that he somehow threatened us and instinctively began to fear him. Yet, when I walked back to him his appearance instilled little apprehension in me. His manner was uncertain, vague and distant. It reassured me against my every instinct. I even had, for a moment, the absurd impression that he was afraid of us. And this flattered my childhood pride.

'My mother says she coming,' I told him.

He said thanks softly. My mother walked out of the door, then stopped and continued to stare at him. He walked towards her and stopped a few yards away. A conspiracy of silence seemed to reign between them, between us I should say, for by now I too was left simply staring, wondering what it was all about. It was he who finally broke the silence.

'Hi, Gladys. I hope I didn't surprise you too much.?'

'How you find where I live?' Her voice was unusually restrained, though there was an ever so slight note of threat in it.

'Oh, I was jus' passing through the town. I ask at the Chinaman shop if they know you, an' they show me the way. . . . '

After another long pause she beckoned to him to come inside. The door remained half-closed and I remained staring at it for the next fifteen minutes. Then I heard my mother calling me. My heart leapt at the thought of finally solving the mystery of the stranger. I found myself stuffing my shirt into my trousers respectfully. My mother

called me again, impatiently. I ran inside.

He was sitting on the only chair we had; she was on the edge of the bed. They both looked at me as I entered. I made sure to avoid his eyes, staring at her for refuge. Then after another long pause, she beckoned to him hesitantly and mumbled, 'Your father.'

I was a little surprised, of course, but not shocked. Perhaps more confused than anything else. I had known he existed somewhere in some shape. But my conception of him had been vague, formless. He had been part of my own personal folk-lore: something I had liked and at times dreamt about, like expensive gold-fish, but never really desired, never took quite seriously. Seeing him there before me, I was sure I would have been no less confounded had I been faced with Humpty-Dumpty. What could I say? What was I expected to

say? They expected me to look at him. Well, I looked at him.

He had lines on his brow and his cheeks were rough. I thought he must shave every day; my friends had told me their fathers did. I thought it would have been very funny if my mother had had to shave every day too; I was not unconscious of my stupid notion.

He nodded in a gesture of approval as he stared at me.

'You are a fine boy,' he said; and I wondered what he meant. Then he looked at my mother and in the same uncertain, unconvincing voice, he repeated, 'He's a fine boy.'

My mother murmured something in response, then glanced at me. Her eyes lacked the proud gleam of satisfaction which they usually bore when someone flattered me in this manner. Instead, they were slightly censorious: I could detect a hint of anger in them and I felt lost to explain why she should have reacted in this manner. When she looked away she held down her head, and if I hadn't known her so well I would have been convinced that there was shame in her eyes. After that she rested her elbow on her knee and her chin between her fingers and sighed, which I knew was her silent, physical way of repeating an expression that was always on her lips: 'Oh, what a life, my God!'

I kept wondering what was going on. I had observed adults to act in the strangest way before; but underlying my ignorance, there had always been some gleam of understanding, awareness, if ever so remote, that whatever they were up to was somehow meaningful. But the behaviour of my mother and the stranger now completely baffled me. Why didn't they say something? Did they hate each other? Did the fact that he was my father mean all that much to her?

Suddenly, I was overwhelmed with the fear that he had come to take her away from me. Perhaps it was that which was worrying them. They did not know how to tell me. My mother would be leaving me all alone. In an instant, the essence of my relationship with her, the importance of her presence, impressed itself on me. I neither loved her nor hated her. I feared her a little, perhaps, for often she would beat me cruelly. But the rage I expressed then in my tears was purely an immediate reaction to the pain I felt. Somehow I conceived that beating me had meant far more to her that it had to me. The world was tough; so she often told me. I was her child and completely at her mercy; it was only natural. Despite everything, a strong bond held us together. Nothing positive, really; more the fear that if we lost each other we would have lost everything. For me she was the person I called mother: she gave me food, clothes and the books I read at school. And she taught me to be good. It was never quite clear what she meant by being good. More often than not, it simply meant *being good* to her, or not being ungrateful, which amounted to much the same thing. I suppose she could be said to have been warm in her own way. But unconsciously, she taught me not to expect very much and so I asked for very little. All I desired was for her to be there, always there. Now there was the threat of her departure.

But that was not possible. I reassured myself that I was being silly to the point of deciding that it would have been better if I left the room. Perhaps they wished to say adult things. As soon as I began to nudge my way to the door I heard him saying, in a manner which suggested that he was repeating himself, 'Yes, it's been a long time, Gladys.' I decided then that I was certainly the reason for their apparent discomfort, and I began to move less imperceptibly to the door. Suddenly I heard my mother call my name. Her voice was sharp and severe; she did not have to say that I must stay; her tone was enough.

The stranger looked at me quizzically, then back at her and suddenly sprang out of his chair. He made the usual motions which indicated an intention to depart; yet, he hesitated. Then he suddenly seemed to remember something. He took out a five-shilling note from his trouser pocket and handed it to me.

'Buy a present with it,' he said.

I stared at the note, a little shocked, both at the large sum of money and at the fact that he, of all people, should have given it to me. I looked up at my mother to see what her response was. I was not surprised when she said, 'I bring 'im up all this time without your help; I don't need it now.'

I immediately held the money out to him for I realised that my mother was in no mood to be crossed. I began to dread the moment when I would be alone with her.

The man began to protest, but he broke off suddenly and took back the note from me. I began to feel sorry for him, for he seemed insulted and sad. He took up his little felt hat, put it on his head and left without saying another word. I never saw him again.

H. ORLANDO PATTERSON

Understanding

1 What do we learn about the boy's relationship with his mother from the story?

2 How much can we tell about Gladys's feelings during the visit? Make it clear in your answer what you are using as evidence from the story.

3 This is a bewildering and worrying time for the boy: his impressions of his father keep changing and often he does not understand the situation. Say at which points in the story the boy seems most confused and explain what it is that is confusing him.

4 How much sympathy do you think Orlando Patterson meant us to have for the boy's father? What are the details the author has included in the story that help decide how readers will feel about the man?

Response

Answer one of the following:

H. Orlando Patterson is Jamaican and you will have noticed that his characters speak in a West Indian dialect. Unless you are very familiar with this form of speech, it is better not to try copying it. Of course this does not stop you producing good work on these exercises.

 1 The author says he never saw his father again, but suppose the two do in fact meet up some years later and that they talk over the visit described in the story. The father explains why he called on Gladys and how he felt at the time, whilst the boy, now a young man, speaks about his own thoughts and feelings that day.

Write their conversation, basing your work on what you have learnt from the story. You may want to try this as a play; if so, read the suggestions on pages 124 and 125.

 2 We are told that the boy's parents were in the house together for fifteen minutes before he was called; and we are also told that because of the mood his mother was in, he was dreading being alone with her when his father left.

Invent these two scenes, making use of what you know or can guess from the story.

Answer one of the following:

1 We are given the occasional clue about the relationship between Gladys and the boy's father some years before, but no details. Write a story about this earlier period in her life that helps the reader understand her involvement with the man, how she felt about him then and why she is now bringing up their child alone.

2 We gather that the boy in the story sometimes found the behaviour of adults strange and on this occasion it completely baffled him. Young children often feel like this. There is a lot about older people they just cannot fathom.

   Think back to your much younger days, to times when 'grown-ups' used to puzzle you too, and write a child's eye view of the adult world, trying to show what an odd place it seemed to you then. You may want to describe one particular occasion, as Orlando Patterson does, or to deal with the topic more generally.

3 Write a story with the title 'A Face from the Past' in which someone turns up unexpectedly and arouses interesting, perhaps disturbing, feelings in you.

17
A PLACE TO STAY

Shelter, the pressure group for the homeless, estimates that at least 150,000 young people aged sixteen to nineteen experience homelessness each year, more than 50,000 of them in London. What follows is taken from a report published recently by Shelter.

Britain has the fastest growing youth homelessness problem in Western Europe. Unlike many other countries where homelessness has risen dramatically, such as Jamaica and Bangladesh, Britain's problem is not due to a natural disaster like a hurricane or a flood. Instead, young people are homeless as a result of new government housing and social security legislation, legislation that has created youth poverty on a scale not seen here since Victorian times.

- Benefit payments to young homeless people have been drastically cut, and are now paid in arrears instead of advance. This means that young people have to survive for up to two weeks without money, and thereafter are constantly in debt. 16- and 17-year-olds are no longer entitled to claim benefits except for a limited period and under certain circumstances; instead they are expected to join a YTS scheme. But young homeless people are often unable to join a scheme and thousands of young people who have registered for YTS are still waiting for a place.

- Grants enabling young homeless people to move into Bed and Breakfast Hotels have been abolished, and replaced with discretionary loans which are usually refused.

- Hostels are being put under such severe pressure by the growing crisis that they are having to turn young people away. They are also having to impose strict time limits on how long young homeless people can stay.

- Permanent accommodation is becoming impossible to find. Rents are rocketing, whilst young homeless people are no longer able to claim grants for rent deposits, advance rent payments, furniture and essential household items.

The legislation is based upon a belief that young people should remain with their parents, until such time as they can afford permanent accommodation. But this is just not an option for many young people.

Thousands leave local authority care every year and have no parents to go back to, thousands more leave their parents because of the stresses of poverty and unemployment. Young lesbians and gay men are often asked to leave when they disclose their sexuality. And many young homeless people are victims of physical and sexual abuse, or come from families where their parents have divorced and are living with new partners, unwilling to keep young people with them after they have left school.

In the past no-one knew what happened to young people once they left their parents or local authority care. So in Autumn 1988 we issued diaries through advice centres and day centres, asking young homeless people to tell us where they spent their time and how much money they had over a 30-day period. The findings, which give a clear picture of young homeless people's lives for the first time, are horrific.

1 A 16-year-old woman from Seven Oaks, in London for 3 months

DAY 1 _____

Today I stayed up the embankment. I can't sign on because I'm 16. I have to go on YTS, but I'm homeless so I can't.

DAY 2 _____

Went begging today, bought a cheeseburger and some fags. Stayed in car park at Euston Station.

DAY 3 _____

Got arrested early hours of this morning for being abusive to a copper. Wow! Got out of the cells 3 hours later.

DAY 4 _____

Met a reporter today who give me £15 for giving her a story on homelessness. Wow! Bought a pizza.

DAY 5 _____

Still got £5 from yesterday and bought some chips. Still staying in Euston but having hassle from police. Might have to move up Embankment tomorrow.

DAY 6 _____

What a bad day! Got smacked in gob by drunk yuppie, spent all night in hospital, St Thomas's.

DAY 7 _____

Got a fat lip. Can't eat as mouth hurts.

DAY 8 _____

Lip a bit better. Ate some chips again. Still up Embankment.

DAY 9 _____

Begged up £6. Ate sausage, beans and chips. Got no sleep up Embankment, a Shaggy went mad and kept us awake all night.

DAY 10 _____

Fed up today. Had enough.

DAY 11 _____

I want to go home, Mum won't have me. Embankment.

DAY 12 _____

No money, got a cold.

DAY 14 _____

Got bad cough as well. Lost my voice.

DAY 16 _____

Found a squat with some mates up Euston today. Ate some chips.

DAY 19 _____

My mate took an OD last night, had had enough. Is in serious state. Poor Gaz!

DAY 20 _____

Gaz a bit better today but still in hospital. Ate chips.

DAY 21 _____

The squat got busted last night and the police have evicted us.

DAY 22 _____

Slept up Temple last night, quite warm.

DAY 24 _____

Felt really ill today, don't know what's wrong. Went to doctor, he said I need to find a home.

2 A 17-year-old man from Bradford, in London for 15 months

DAY 2
Sat in Leicester Square half the day, then went looking for work again on a building site. The money is good on building sites, because the work is hard, and I went begging for my tea and supper. Didn't make much money though, it was a very bad day indeed.

DAY 4
Going for a job interview today. I am just praying that I get it.

DAY 6
Walking down to the DHSS again to ask for a crisis loan, because I need it badly now.

DAY 7
Going to try and find another hostel today that is better than Riverpoint (an emergency night shelter).

DAY 9
Thinking of going down to Heathrow to steal some aftershave, then you can sell it for about £10.

DAY 12
I did not find a hostel, so slept in Leicester Square. It was freezing cold, even though I had a sleeping bag.

DAY 13
I might be going home to Bradford soon to see my friends. I really miss them, and my family.

DAY 14
Went to DHSS again, but no luck with my claim. They just get on my nerves all the time.

DAY 15
Just going to sit about all day drinking beer because I have been begging again, did quite good today.

DAY 20
No money, no food, now I feel really bad. Going begging, hope I make a lot of money.

DAY 21
Going to the doctor's because my health is bad now, really bad.

DAY 23
Didn't find nowhere to stay again, going to sleep in the square again tonight.

DAY 24
I am seriously thinking of leaving London now, it's getting me down all the time.

EXTRACTS FROM THE DIARIES

3 A 19-year-old woman from Lincoln, in London for 8 months

DAY 4

Dave my boyfriend mugged someone and we went shopping for food.

DAY 5

Bought a £10 draw and got smashed, there's nothing else to do. Tried the Job Centre, nothing there.

DAY 6

Went looking for a squat today. A few possible sites in Tottenham and Stamford Hill, but can't move in yet.

DAY 9

Got benefit. Went out for a drink and got arrested for drunk and disorderly. Court tomorrow.

DAY 10

Court today. £40 fine and there's no money left as Davey has spent it all. Slept in Leicester Square.

DAY 11

Hanging round the square all day. Was offered a job in Soho as a hostess. The way things are going I might take it. Slept in square.

DAY 14

We moved into the squat in Stoke Newington.

DAY 15

Made a fresh claim today, it will take 2 weeks to get any money. Started working the beat at Kings Cross as I need the money. Got a couple of punters and went home.

DAY 16

Went to work, got a punter and got arrested for soliciting. Court in the morning.

DAY 17

Another £40 fine and 1 year's probation. Centrepoint (a short-stay night shelter) for the night.

DAY 18

Picked up a couple of punters. Slept at one of their houses.

DAY 19

Stayed in bed all day. I am physically exhausted. Got a Chinese takeaway. Dave knows I am a prostitute and he doesn't mind as long as he gets half.

DAY 20

Went to work today and got beat up. No point in calling the police, they won't do anything.

4 A 17-year-old man from Manchester, in London for 12 months

DAY 3

I slept rough in Leicester Square, an agonising night this time.

DAY 4

I have been getting into fights while I'm living rough on the streets. It is beyond a joke now. I would like to have my own flat, that would be very nice right now, with my girlfriend living there as well.

DAY 5

I have been playing frisbee in St James Park today, it was pretty good, better than sitting about all day doing nothing. I like frisbees a lot, and skateboarding, it's fascinating.

DAY 6

I am starting to run out of clean clothes now, and I have no money to go to the launderette. I would like a nice hot bath and some clean clothes right now.

DAY 7

I might be applying for a job today on a building site. Then I will get a Bed and Breakfast.

DAY 8

I want some money so I can buy some new clothes, I am starting to look really scruffy now, and my girlfriend looks very smart. I don't want to show her up walking with her, it is not really fair on her.

DAY 9

I could do with a stereo to listen to at night before I go to sleep on my park bench. I am quite warm in my sleeping bag at night, it is quite nice.

DAY 12

I really want to be reunited with my family again if I can. I really would like it very much. I still love my mother very much and the rest of the family, even though I don't live there.

DAY 13

I am really getting sick of doing the same old thing every day.

1 According to Shelter, what is wrong with the government's idea of discouraging young people from leaving home before they can support themselves properly?

2 Pressure groups like Shelter are sometimes accused of pushing anti-government propaganda based merely on the political opinions they happen to hold. Would you say the criticisms expressed in the introduction on page 107 are mainly matters of opinion or matters of fact? Give clear reasons for your answer.

3 After reading the diary extracts, what seem to you to be the most serious dangers young people face living rough in London?

4 Although the extracts are short, we can see that they are written by four very different people. Decide which two of the diarists seem most unlike each other in their personalities and attitudes, and explain clearly what you think are the differences between them.

Answer one of the following:

1 People who read the diaries will react to them in different ways. Some will have no patience at all with the teenagers who wrote them, whilst others will be extremely understanding. Imagine you are a reader of the first sort and describe your reactions to the extracts, then repeat the exercise, this time as a much more sympathetic reader. In both cases, tie your remarks closely to what is actually said in the diaries.

2 A letter from a friend includes this paragraph:
I've had enough of things at home − all the arguments and everything. The moment I leave school next June, I'm off. Down to London. I've got to get away from all this. I know I'll manage by myself somehow.

You have read pages 106 to 112, so this letter worries you: does the writer really understand the sort of life people on their own can lead in London, and the difficulties and dangers they face?
   Write a reply, tactfully advising your friend to think carefully before rushing into something he or she might regret. Your letter should make use of what you have learnt in the Shelter report and the diaries.
   Read the suggestions on page 122 before you begin.

3 Although the diaries make a strong impression on the reader, the entries are usually very short. Often we can only

guess exactly how the writers spent their days and what their feelings were.

Imagine you are one of these young people and write three longer, more detailed diary entries. The first entry should have been written just before you leave for London, the second very soon after you arrive and the third some weeks later. Basing your work on the Shelter material, try to show how your feelings change as your hopes for a new life in the capital come up against the realities you find there.

Your writing

Answer one of the following:

1   Three of the diarists say they want to go back to see people at home. These reunions might work, but, of course, they could be terribly disappointing.

Write a short story based on the idea of 'going back': for example, back to family and friends, taking the case of one of the diarists perhaps, or maybe back to a place that holds special memories or to see someone who, though not a friend, used to play an important part in your life. Develop the idea in any way you think will interest the reader.

2   One thing that might strike you about the diarists is their perseverance. They manage to hold out for months in the face of terrible problems.

Write either about times in your own life when you have had to force yourself to keep going despite difficulties that made you want to give up; or about people you know or know of whose perseverance has impressed you.

3   However happy you are at present, you almost certainly look forward to becoming independent sooner or later and setting up a home of your own, and you probably have a fair idea of the kind of place you would like this to be.

Imagine you already have the home of your dreams and describe it in some detail, explaining what it is you love about it.

Rita left school with no qualifications. In her mid-twenties and unhappy in her job as a hairdresser, she begins a Literature course with the Open University, which caters for older, part-time students. Frank is her tutor and in his forties.

The lights come up on Frank who is sitting in the armchair in his office listening to the radio.
Rita enters, goes straight to the desk and slings her bag on the back of her chair. She sits in the chair and unpacks the note-pad and pencil-case from her bag. She opens the pad and takes out the pencils and arranges them. Frank gets up, switches off the radio, goes to the swivel chair and sits.

FRANK   Now *I* don't mind; two empty seats at the dinner table means more of the vino for me. But Julia — Julia is the stage-manager type. If we're having eight people to dinner she expects to see eight. She likes order — probably why she took me in — it gives her a lot of practice —

(Rita starts sharpening her pencils.)

FRANK   — and having to cope with six instead of eight was extremely hard on Julia. I'm not saying that I needed any sort of apology; you don't turn up that's up to you, but . . .

RITA   I did apologise.

FRANK   'Sorry couldn't come', scribbled on the back of your essay and thrust through the letter box? Rita, that's hardly an apology.

RITA   What does the word 'sorry' mean if it's not an apology? When I told Denny we were goin' to yours he went mad. We had a big fight about it.

FRANK   I'm sorry. I didn't realize. But look, couldn't you have explained? Couldn't you have said that was the reason?

RITA   No. Cos that wasn't the reason. I told Denny if he wasn't gonna go I'd go on me own. An' I tried to. All day Saturday, all day in the shop I was thinkin' what to wear. I got back, an' I tried on five different dresses. They all looked bleedin' awful. An' all the time I'm trying to think of things I can say, what I can talk about. An' I can't remember anythin'. It's all jumbled up in me head. I can't remember if it's Wilde who's witty an' Shaw who was Shavian or who the hell wrote *Howards End.**

FRANK   Oh God!

RITA   Then I got the wrong bus to your house. It took me ages to find it. Then I walked up your drive, an' I saw y'all through the window, y'were sippin' drinks an' talkin' an' laughin'. An' I couldn't come in.

FRANK   Of course you could.

* Wilde and Shaw are famous writers. *Howards End* is by the British novelist, E.M. Forster.

RITA   I couldn't. I'd bought the wrong sort of wine. When I was in the off licence I knew I was buying the wrong stuff. But I didn't know which was the right wine.

FRANK   Rita for Christ's sake; I wanted *you* to come along. You weren't expected to dress up or buy wine.

RITA   (*holding all the pencils and pens in her hands and playing with them.*)If you go out to dinner don't you dress up? Don't you take wine?

FRANK   Yes, but . . .

RITA   Well?

FRANK   Well what?

RITA   Well you wouldn't take sweet sparkling wine, would y'?

FRANK   Does it matter what I do? It wouldn't have mattered if you'd walked in with a bottle of Spanish plonk.

RITA   It *was* Spanish.

FRANK   Why couldn't you relax?
(*He gets up and goes behind Rita's chair, then leans on the back of it.*)It wasn't a fancy dress party. You could have come as yourself. Don't you realise how people would have seen you if you'd just − just breezed in? Mm? They would have seen someone who's funny, delightful, charming . . .

RITA   (*angrily*) But I don't wanna be charming and delightful: funny. What's funny? I don't wanna be funny. I wanna talk seriously with the rest of you, I don't wanna spend the night comin' on with the funnies because that's the only way I can get into the conversation. I didn't want to come to your house just to play the court jester.

FRANK   You weren't being asked to play that role. I just — just wanted you to be yourself.

RITA   But I don't want to be myself. Me? What's me? Some stupid woman who gives us all a laugh because she thinks she can learn, because she thinks that one day she'll be like the rest of them, talking seriously, confidently, with knowledge, livin' a civilized life. Well, she can't be like that really but bring her in because she's good for a laugh!

FRANK   If you believe that's why you were invited, to be laughed at, then you can get out, now. (*He goes to his desk and grabs a pile of essays, taking them to the window desk. He stands with his back to Rita and starts pushing them into his briefcase.*) You were invited because I wished to have your company and if you can't believe that then I suggest you stop visiting me and start visiting a psychiatrist.

RITA   I'm all right with you in this room; but when I saw those people you were with I couldn't come in. I would have seized up. Because I'm a freak. I can't talk to the people I live with any more. An' I can't talk to the likes of them on Saturday, or the students out there, because I can't learn the language. I'm a half-caste. I went back to the pub where Denny was, an' me mother an' our Sandra, an' her mates. I'd decided I wasn't comin' here again. (*Frank turns to face her.*)

RITA   I went into the pub an' they were singin', all of them singin' some song they'd learnt from the juke-box. An' I stood in that pub an' thought, just what am I trying to do? Why don't I pack it in an' stay with them, an' join in the singin'?

FRANK   And why don't you?

RITA   (*angrily*) You think I can, don't you? Just because you pass a pub doorway an' hear the singin' you think we're all O.K., that we're all survivin', with the spirit intact. Well I did join in with the singin', I didn't ask any questions, I just went along with it. But when I looked round me mother had stopped singin', an' she was cryin', but no one could get it out of her why she was cryin'. Everyone just said she was drunk an' we should get her home. So we did, an' on the way I asked her why. I said, 'Why are y'cryin', Mother?' She said, 'Because — because we could sing better songs than those.' Ten minutes later, Denny had her laughing and singing again, pretending she hadn't said it. But she had. And that's why I came back. And that's why I'm staying. (*Rita goes out.*)

Willy Russell
Educating Rita

THE CHOOSING

We were first equal Mary and I
with the same coloured ribbons in mouse-coloured hair
and with equal shyness,
we curtseyed to the lady councillor
for copies of Collins' Children's Classics.
First equal, equally proud.

Best friends too Mary and I
a common bond in being cleverest (equal)
in our small school's small class.
I remember
the competition for top desk
or to read aloud the lesson
at school service.
And my terrible fear
of her superiority at sums.

I remember the housing scheme
where we both stayed.
The same houses, different homes,
where the choices were made.

I don't know exactly why they moved,
but anyway they went.
Something about a three-apartment
and a cheaper rent.
But from the top deck of the high-school bus
I'd glimpse among the others on the corner
Mary's father, mufflered, contrasting strangely with
the elegant greyhounds by his side.
He didn't believe in high school education,
especially for girls,
or in forking out for uniforms.

Ten years later on a Saturday —
I am coming from the library —
sitting near me on the bus,
Mary
with a husband who is tall,
curly haired, has eyes
for no one else but Mary.
Her arms are round the full-shaped vase
that is her body.
Oh, you can see where the attraction lies
in Mary's life —
not that I envy her, really.

And I am coming from the library
with my arms full of books.
I think of those prizes that were ours for the taking
and I wonder when the choices got made
we don't remember making.

LIZ LOCHHEAD

Rita's and Frank's emotions run high at several points. Even before they begin speaking we can see they are both upset, and later Rita in her last speech on page 116 'But I don't wanna . . .' and Frank in his second speech on page 117 'If you believe . . .' become very heated. Their feelings are shown not only in what they say but also in *how* they express themselves and in their physical actions.

Study the three places in the scene just mentioned and then in each case say briefly why Frank and/or Rita feel so strongly and explain how they show their feelings in the way they speak and the things they do.

Rita tells Frank, 'I'd decided I wasn't comin' here again' in the middle of page 117. Why did Rita make this decision to stop her course and why did she later change her mind and decide to continue?

To answer these questions well you will need to think carefully about the reasons Rita gives for not attending Frank's party and what she says about the incident with her mother afterwards.

Referring closely to the way Frank and Rita speak and behave to each other in the scene, say whether theirs is the sort of relationship we would normally expect between teacher and student.

In the first few lines of the poem *The Choosing*, 'equal' is repeated several times. In what ways were the girls equal at that stage in their lives and why do you think the poet wants to stress that word?

As young women, Mary and Liz have grown apart but the poet cannot remember them actually *choosing* to go different ways. Describe their two life-styles at the end of the poem, and say whether the poem helps us understand how the differences came about.

Answer one of the following:

Near the start of the passage, Rita refers to a scene that does not actually appear in the play: the row she had with her husband, Denny, when she told him they had been invited to Frank's party.

Invent this scene, basing it on what we know from the passage about Rita and her feelings and the little we learn about Denny. Use the same layout as the extract and, before you start, read the suggestions on writing a play which you will find on pages 124 and 125.

2 Suppose that Rita is a friend of yours and has written to you describing the difficulties she has met since she began the Open University course. Reply to this letter, referring to her particular problems and offering whatever advice you think will help her.

3 Imagine the girls in Liz Lochhead's poem had spoken to each other on the bus about their time together at primary school and what they have done since. Do you think they would have enjoyed the meeting or might it have been spoilt by feelings of envy and embarrassment?

When you have decided this question, write your own version of their conversation, perhaps describing it from Mary's point of view.

Your writing

Answer one of the following:

1 Rita says, 'I'm a half-caste' on page 117 because she thinks she no longer fully belongs to any of the groups of people she knows. She feels she is an outsider, isolated and alone. Write a short story in which, for whatever reason, someone goes through this same sense of loneliness and isolation.

2 'But I don't want to be myself. Me? What's me?' Most of us have felt like Rita at one time or another. What is there about yourself that you sometimes wish you could change?

3 These are some of the questions raised by *Educating Rita* and *The Choosing* :

If you can find a well paid job at sixteen, is there any real point staying on at school or college?

What do people get out of studying 'useless' subjects like Literature?

Is education just as important for girls as it is for boys?

What are your views on one or more of these questions? Explain clearly the reasons for your opinions.

News Articles

Bold, striking headlines capture our attention.

The opening paragraphs 'sell' us the story by highlighting its most exciting details.

We are now given the full story.

Quotations from interviews are reassuring: we have more than just the reporter's word for what happened.

Short sub-headings taken from later in the article encourage us to continue reading.

COPS CLUB DOG TO DEATH IN ACID RAID

Devil hound terror

TERRIFIED police were forced to kill a savage pit-bull terrier set on them at a wild Acid House party.

They beat the brutal beast to death with truncheons and clubs as it tried to attack them, it was revealed last night.

Acid House organisers let the dog loose when 180 police — many in riot gear — stormed a disused warehouse.

As tempers rose among the 3,000 partygoers thug bouncers threatened officers with rottweilers and dobermanns.

"But one of them actually let the pit-bull terrier loose and we were forced to kill it for our own safety," said a policeman on the scene.

Knives

"We had to club it to death with our truncheons. It was ghastly, but they forced us to do it. These dogs are lethal."

Police arrested 45 revellers as spaced-out youths

EXCLUSIVE by MARK CHRISTY

high on ecstasy went wild at the warehouse on the Riverway Industrial Estate in Harlow, Essex.

Cocaine, LSD, heroin and ecstasy were seized as well as a stash of flick-knifes, clubs, claw hammers and a knuckle-duster.

Last night Essex Police spokesman Roy Clark confirmed the pit-bull terrier horror.

"The dog attacked our officers," he said.

Narrow columns and short paragraphs are easier to read.

- Journalists can make quite ordinary events seem interesting, even to people who do not much enjoy reading. They do this by stressing the most dramatic features of a story and describing these in a 'punchy', gripping way; for example, in this article the dog is said to be *savage, brutal* and *lethal,* its death was *ghastly,* the party was *wild* and the police *stormed* the building.

- Not everyone approves of this sort of 'sensationalist' journalism. Some prefer a calmer, fuller and more factual version of events, and there are, of course, newspapers which cater for this taste.

A Personal Letter

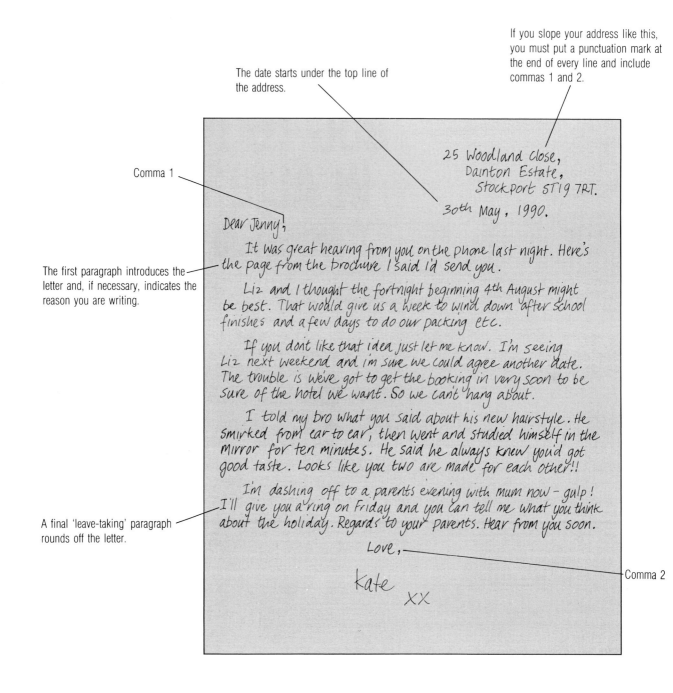

If you slope your address like this, you must put a punctuation mark at the end of every line and include commas 1 and 2.

The date starts under the top line of the address.

Comma 1

The first paragraph introduces the letter and, if necessary, indicates the reason you are writing.

A final 'leave-taking' paragraph rounds off the letter.

Comma 2

> 25 Woodland Close,
> Dainton Estate,
> Stockport ST19 7RT.
> 30th May, 1990.
>
> Dear Jenny,
>
> It was great hearing from you on the phone last night. Here's the page from the brochure I said I'd send you.
>
> Liz and I thought the fortnight beginning 4th August might be best. That would give us a week to wind down after school finishes and a few days to do our packing etc.
>
> If you don't like that idea just let me know. I'm seeing Liz next weekend and im sure we could agree another date. The trouble is we've got to get the booking in very soon to be sure of the hotel we want. So we can't hang about.
>
> I told my bro what you said about his new hairstyle. He smirked from ear to ear, then went and studied himself in the mirror for ten minutes. He said he always knew you'd got good taste. Looks like you two are made for each other!!
>
> I'm dashing off to a parents evening with mum now – gulp! I'll give you a ring on Friday and you can tell me what you think about the holiday. Regards to your parents. Hear from you soon.
>
> Love,
>
> Kate
> xx

- Dividing up the letter into several paragraphs makes it easier and more pleasant to read.

- The style of the writing in a personal letter is informal and friendly – more like ordinary speech, in fact.

A Formal Letter

If you use this 'blocked' layout for your address, punctuation is not needed and there are no commas in the date or after *Dear Sir* and *Yours faithfully*. You do not punctuate the receiver's address either.

```
                              14 Broadmead Road
                              Parkside
                              Tenby
                              TN27 96S

                              14th July 1990


Your reference: 6H/9

The Manager
Audio Rentals Ltd
127 Pembroke Road
Tenby
TN14 8PD

Dear Sir

Thank you for your letter dated 11th July in which you inform me
that you have not received my rental payment for June.

I am puzzled by what you say.  I have been in touch with my bank
and they confirm that the standing order for £12.85 was paid to
you on 10th June.

I can only assume that your accounts department has somehow
overlooked the payment. May I ask you to check again and let me
know the outcome?

I look forward to hearing from you soon.

Yours faithfully


J. Manners
```

The receiver's address. Each line begins at the margin, whether or not you have used the blocked layout for your own address.

If you had started with the receiver's name — for example, *Dear Mr Jones* — you would end *Yours sincerely.*

- In this sort of letter the writing is business-like and quite formal. You would not normally use shortened forms (*I'm, it's* and so on) or 'conversational' expressions of the kind found in the personal letter — *give you a ring* and *can't hang around,* for example.

Writing A Script

Space kept for the names of characters about to speak.

The scene is briefly set before the actors begin speaking.

Instructions to actors about what to do when they are not speaking are given lines of their own, separate from the speech.

Instructions about how actors should say their lines or what they should do while speaking are left in with the speech itself.

All these instructions are underlined and in brackets so that actors know they are not to be spoken.

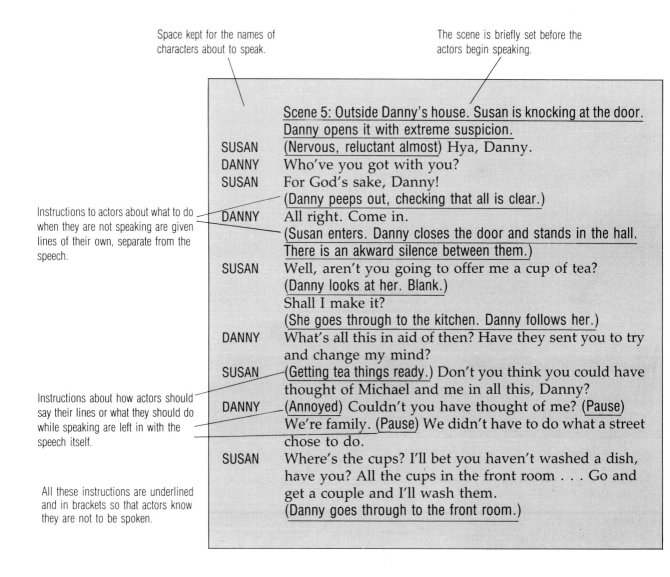

Scene 5: Outside Danny's house. Susan is knocking at the door. Danny opens it with extreme suspicion.

SUSAN   (Nervous, reluctant almost) Hya, Danny.

DANNY   Who've you got with you?

SUSAN   For God's sake, Danny!
(Danny peeps out, checking that all is clear.)

DANNY   All right. Come in.
(Susan enters. Danny closes the door and stands in the hall. There is an akward silence between them.)

SUSAN   Well, aren't you going to offer me a cup of tea?
(Danny looks at her. Blank.)
Shall I make it?
(She goes through to the kitchen. Danny follows her.)

DANNY   What's all this in aid of then? Have they sent you to try and change my mind?

SUSAN   (Getting tea things ready.) Don't you think you could have thought of Michael and me in all this, Danny?

DANNY   (Annoyed) Couldn't you have thought of me? (Pause) We're family. (Pause) We didn't have to do what a street chose to do.

SUSAN   Where's the cups? I'll bet you haven't washed a dish, have you? All the cups in the front room . . . Go and get a couple and I'll wash them.
(Danny goes through to the front room.)

- Aim to make your dialogue sound natural — the way people really do speak. So, for example, it will not always be in complete, polished sentences.

- Because we are all different, we talk differently; try to get your characters to show the type of people they are through their speech.

- Remember your dialogue is telling a story and stories must be interesting. There should always be something *happening* between the characters: they may be arguing or making up, one may be trying to bully, persuade or calm the other, they may be expressing strong feelings or struggling to hide them − in other words, we need more than just pointless chit-chat.

You will find that the layout on the opposite page works for stage, radio and most television scripts. But if you are writing a TV news item or a documentary, you may need to use the directions 'V/O' and 'SYNC':

V/O means 'voice over': the voice is not someone speaking on the screen.

(Film: scene of aircrash. Wreckage strewn over wide area. Police, firemen and airport workers engaged in clear-up operation.)

V/O
JOHN
SHAW

Air Holland Flight 457 took off from Woodness Airport soon after ten this morning. It was bound for Amsterdam with 146 people on board.
(Film: Margaret Leeson. Exterior.)

V/O
JOHN

Airport worker Margaret Leeson witnessed what happened next.

SYNC
MARGARET

The plane had just cleared the trees over there when there was this almighty explosion. A ball of flame shot out of one of the engines and the plane exploded. It just fell out of the sky.
(Film: scene of crash as before.)

'SYNC' means the voice is synchronised with the picture: the person or one of the people on the screen is speaking.

V/O
JOHN

The aircraft hit the ground in several sections one mile from the end of the main runway. Emergency services were on the . . .

Six Ways to Write Better Stories

1 **Before you begin** Story-writing is a pointless exercise unless you aim to *affect* your readers; and you must be clear how you intend to do this before you begin writing. For example, you could decide you want them to imagine they are living through some terrifying experience; or to feel how awful it is to lose someone they love; or to smile at some ridiculous incident.

   Whatever your intention, it must be in your mind at the start and you must never lose sight of it; everything you write should be helping you in some way or other to do what you have set out to do.

2 **Selecting your material** It follows that you must not add dead weight to your story by padding it out with irrelevant facts. How your characters earn their living, what they had for breakfast, their conversation about the weather − unless this sort of information contributes something useful to the story, leave it out.

3 **How you put your story together** The most obvious way of telling a story is to begin at the beginning and work through events in the order they occurred till you reach the end:

But there are other possibilities you might try. For example, you could start near the end and then fill in the earlier part of the story with a series of 'flashbacks':

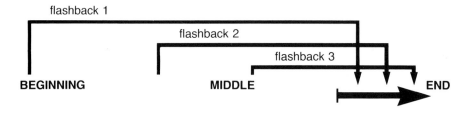

For example, a prisoner, waiting for the jury to return with its verdict, might think over the events that brought him to court.

4 The opening Get the story under way in the first few lines – preferably in the very first sentence, which should be one that immediately engages the readers' attention. These openings are by two well-known writers and both of them draw us straight into the action:

> *Everything began to be better for Mrs Reinhardt from the moment she started to sleepwalk. (Edna O'Brien)*
> *Captain Hart stood in the door of the rocket. 'Why don't they come?' he said. (Ray Bradbury)*

5 Showing, not telling Your readers will not be satisfied if you merely *inform* them that something happened: you need to *show* them it taking place. For example, Wilbur Smith does not simply tell us: 'The wounded lion attacked the men', instead he writes this picture into our minds:

> *He came straight at them out of the thicket as his mate had done, but even more swiftly, driven by the agony in his belly and the black rage that filled him. He came grunting like a locomotive at full throttle, and they were unprepared, their rifles unloaded, bunched too closely around the carcass of the lioness, and Shadrack was between them and the lion.*

When you are trying to create suspense in your story, it is particularly important that you slow down the action and describe it in detail.

6 The ending There are many ways to end a story but no easy rules to help you decide how it should be done. Luckily most of us just know when a story finishes well, though we cannot always say what it is we like about it. However, you should remember these points:

- When you reach the end, stop! This may seem obvious but stories are often allowed to drag on long after they have reached their natural stopping point. Let your readers tie off the loose ends for themselves.
- Stories do not have to finish happily. In fact, making everything come right in the last paragraph, especially when this happens completely out of the blue, can seem like cheating. Some stories *need* a sad ending; others wisely leave it to the reader to decide how things will turn out.
- Do not feel you must have an unexpected 'twist' at the end. Roald Dahl is one writer who uses this 'sting in the tail' technique very cleverly, but do not feel every story you write must have this sort of ending.

Campaign Leaflets and Advertisements

A dramatic, rather puzzling title encourages us to read on

This striking statistic immediately grabs our attention

WHAT'S IN A LIFE?
In a lifetime, the average British meat-eater eats, 36 pigs, 36 sheep, 8 cattle and 550 poultry. . . .

TAKE DEATH OUT OF YOUR DIET

THE KILLING FIELDS

Every year in the U.K. we slaughter more than 500 million chicken, 15.5 million pigs, 29.5 million turkey, 4 million cattle, 15.5 million sheep and 2.5 million rabbits for food. Contrary to popular opinion they are not 'humanely killed'.

A Report by the governments own Advisory Council (FAWC) criticised 'woeful ignorance' amongst abattoir staff, 'random application of electrodes to the anus or genital area' when moving animals and defective equipment which - in the words of another Meat Industry representative - turns the death of many animals into a 'noisy and doubtless painful nightmare'.

BLOOD, GORE AND MORE

Animal bloodshed is also a human health hazard. An E.E.C. report on British slaughterhouses (1986) found 'a frightening picture of poor hygiene, slapdash organisation and blood and gore all over the floor'.

No wonder severe food poisoning is on the increase. Poultry meat is responsible for 50% of reported incidents of salmonella and red meat a further 20%.

How many of us could slit an animals throat or even watch it being done? Not you? Then why allow others to do the dirty work for you?

A few well chosen facts make out a strong case.
They are clearly and boldly stated — no-one would have any trouble understanding them.

Quotations from independent sources make us more ready to believe the information.

A shocking illustration drives the message home.

Questions like these get us to feel personally involved in the issue.

- The overall design must be eye catching, well spaced and easy to read. Has too much material been crammed into this leaflet? Would it have been better to print the right-hand column of information overleaf?
- Give some thought to how upsetting a leaflet or advert should be. Do you think this one goes too far and needs toning down a little, or is it justified because the issue is so serious?